PROJECT BASED LEARNING
WORKBOOK SERIES

PBL 101 WORKBOOK

The Companion to BIE's Introductory
Project Based Learning Workshop

BUCK INSTITUTE FOR EDUCATION

PROJECT BASED LEARNING
FOR THE 21ST CENTURY

BUCK INSTITUTE FOR EDUCATION

About the Buck Institute for Education

Founded in 1987, the Buck Institute for Education works to expand the effective use of Project Based Learning throughout the world. BIE is a mission-driven not-for-profit 501(c)3 organization based in Novato, California, and is a beneficiary of the Leonard and Beryl Buck Trust. BIE has provided PBL professional development services to thousands of educators, curriculum development consulting, and ongoing support for organizations including school districts, state departments of education, foundations, and other partners in the United States and around the world. BIE hosts annual *PBL World* conferences and *PBL Academies*, and offers online resources at its website and online classes at **PBLU.org**. It published the acclaimed *Project Based Learning Handbook*, and now publishes the *PBL Toolkit Series* of books on how to do PBL. BIE publications have been translated into nine languages.

PBL 101 WORKBOOK

Principal Authors
Alfred Solis
John Larmer
Gina Olabuenaga

We thank very much the many members of the BIE National Faculty who contributed to the design of the 2014 edition of PBL 101 Workshop and Workbook. Your experience, wisdom, professionalism, and dedication to PBL are appreciated.

Published by Buck Institute for Education
18 Commercial Boulevard., Novato, California 94949 USA
www.bie.org

May 2014: Fourth Edition.

Printed by Unicorn Printing Specialists, San Rafael, California.
Printed on acid-free paper with soy-based ink.

Designed by Pam Scrutton, San Francisco, California.

ISBN 978-0-9740343-4-8

PROJECT BASED LEARNING
WORKBOOK SERIES

PBL 101 WORKBOOK

Table of Contents

TABLE OF CONTENTS

Project Path

What Students Think About:

- What is the project asking me to do?
- What do I need to know?
- Why is this important?
- Who will I be sharing my work with?

- What resources can and should I use?
- Can I trust the information I am finding?
- What is my role in the process?

- How can I apply what I have learned to the project?
- What new questions do I have?
- Do I need more information?
- Is my work on the right track?

- What should I explain about my work?
- How can I best share this with others?
- What have I learned and what should I do in the next project?

How Teachers Support Inquiry:

Launch Project: Entry Event + Driving Question

- Conduct Entry Event and present/co-construct Driving Question
- Facilitate process for generating student questions

Build Knowledge, Understanding & Skills to Answer Driving Question

- Facilitate use and evaluation of resources
- Provide lessons, scaffolds, and guidance in response to student needs

Develop and Critique Products and Answers to the Driving Question

- Help students apply learning to project tasks
- Provide additional experiences to generate new knowledge and questions
- Facilitate processes for feedback

Present Products and Answers to the Driving Question

- Help students evaluate their work
- Facilitate student reflection on process and learning

Revision

INTRODUCTION

Welcome to PBL 101. This workshop is designed to teach you the basics of Project Based Learning. By the end we hope you are ready, willing and able to use this effective teaching method with your students.

PBL 101 is designed to mirror the experience of a project, following the basic path of the diagram at left. It begins the way BIE recommends launching a project with students—with an Entry Event that engages you and leads you to ask questions about the task. From there, you will gain knowledge and skills to help you complete the major product of this "project"— a plan you can use to conduct a project in your classroom. There will be checkpoints along the way, assessment of your work, and a presentation.

The workshop has three basic parts: Project Design, Assessment, and Management. At the end of each part is a deliverable—a product or task you will need to complete.

Outcomes

By the end of this workshop, you will have designed a project for your own use.

You will have a better understanding of:

■ The difference between PBL and "doing projects"

■ The need to provide students with opportunities to practice 21st century competencies, balanced with learning significant content

■ How to manage a project in your classroom

The Purpose of This Workbook

The *PBL 101 Workbook* will be used to practice, apply, and extend what you are learning in the workshop. Think of this workbook as "scaffolding" for your project planning process. Like a project, this workbook is open-ended; it is not a script that leads every participant to design the same project. The workshop is an introduction to PBL and is intended to be followed by instructional coaching. Because planning a project is a complex undertaking, you might not have a fully completed project by the end of the workshop. To continue planning your project after the workshop ends, use the resources available at **bie.org** and in BIE publications for further support.

How This Workbook is Organized

This workbook has two main sections: **Tasks** and **Resources**.

Tasks are a combination of written exercises and prompts for activities. They will guide you in thinking through how your project will address the Essential Elements of PBL. Some Tasks are optional, but can be used later with your colleagues or a PBL coach.

Resources include additional readings, tools such as rubrics and planning forms, and materials to be used in workshop activities.

Your workshop facilitator and the presentation slides will prompt you to begin the Tasks in this workbook. Please do NOT peek ahead!

QR Codes

Throughout this workbook you will see QR codes next to items you can find online by scanning the code with your smartphone. You'll be taken right to the location of the item on the **bie.org** website.

Day 1:
DESIGNING PROJECTS

The following tasks are to be completed before the **Charrette**:

- **TASK 1.1 Project Launch**
  - ▶ Part A. Need to Know List
  - ▶ Part B. Project Information Sheet

- **TASK 1.2 Essential Elements Poster**

- **TASK 1.3 Project Search** (optional)

- **TASK 1.4 Getting Started**
  - ▶ Part A. Select Significant Content for Your Project
  - ▶ Part B. Develop a Project Idea
  - ▶ Part C. Decide on Major Student Products
  - ▶ Part D. Involve a Public Audience

- **TASK 1.5 Writing a Driving Question**
  - ▶ Part A. DQ Brainstorm
  - ▶ Part B. Determine Your Driving Question

TASK 1.1 Project Launch ⟵

1. Entry Event - could be a video
2. Driving Question
3. (Students do this) - indiv. + then w/ ea. other

Part A. Need to Know List *(Can add to this always - a "living document")*

Think about what you might need to know in order to complete the challenge you have been given in the Entry Event and answer the Driving Question, How can we plan effective projects for our students? Write your questions below.

☑ *What work is done in class - what out?*

☐ How can I assess critical thinking?

☐ *How do I motivate my students during the project*

☐ *How do I know if they have enough mastery of content to work through the project? (How much "front-loading?)*

☐ *How do I know if my project is engaging to students?*

☐ *How do I teach my students to work together effectively?*

☑ *How do I differentiate?*

☐ *How do I spread out the time - allocate time in class?*

☑ *How do I find a balance in my scaffolding*

☑ *What experts do I need to bring in*

☐ *How do I form groups?*

☑ *What standards do I follow*

☑ *How much freedom do I give students*

☐ *How*

☑ *What formative evaluation do I do*

☐ *What type of assessment or grading do I use?*

☐ *What length of time is most effective*

☐ *What is best way to give meaningful feedback*

☑ *What are the parameters of choice*

☑ *What is important to students right now?*

Reminder

Feel free to add more questions to this list at any point during the workshop. We will revisit it regularly to review what we have learned.

If you have further Need to Knows about PBL, visit **bie.org** and open the "Community" tab, where you will find links to social media networks so you can connect with colleagues, BIE staff and National Faculty.

☑ *Where can I find good resources*

☑ *How can I tie in to the business world?*

©2014 BUCK INSTITUTE FOR EDUCATION

☑ *What does a daily lesson look like -*

Part B. Project Information Sheet

The Project to Begin All Projects

To respond to the request from the students, you will be collaboratively designing one project to use in your own classroom. The project should include BIE's Essential Elements of Project Based Learning and will be presented for critique to an audience of your peers.

Driving Question: How can we plan effective projects for our students?

Major Product: a plan for your project

Duration: 3 days

Deliverables	Due On:
Sh Charrette	end of Day One
Gallery Walk	morning of Day Two
Student Learning Guide	end of Day Two
Critical Friends Protocol	morning of Day Three
Project Design Overview	end of Day Three

Requirements

Day One: Designing Projects Lesson

☐ TASK 1.1 Project Launch

☐ TASK 1.2 Essential Elements Poster

☐ TASK 1.3 Project Search (optional)

☐ TASK 1.4 Getting Started

☐ TASK 1.5 Writing a Driving Question

Day Two: Assessing Projects Lesson

☐ TASK 2.1 High Quality Assessment

☐ TASK 2.2 Assessment Planning (optional)

☐ TASK 2.3 Differentiation Time

Day Three: Managing Projects Lesson

☐ TASK 3.1 Entry Event Planning

☐ TASK 3.2 Project Presentation

☐ TASK 3.3 Collective Wisdom

☐ TASK 3.4 Forming Teams (optional)

☐ TASK 3.5 Über Meta-Moment

Online Resources

Project Search:	**bie.org/project_search**
Useful Downloads:	**bie.org/objects/cat/read**
BIE online communities:	**bie.org/community**
BIE YouTube channel:	**youtube.com/biepbl**

Evaluation Criteria

Project Design Rubric (See *Resources*)

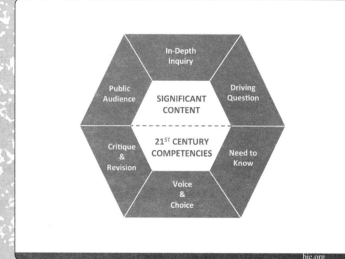

	LIMITED	AMBITIOUS
Duration	10-15 contact hours	20+ contact hours
Breadth	One subject	Interdisciplinary
Who's Involved	One teacher	Several teachers, outside experts, community
Authenticity	Simulates the real world	In or for the real world
Audience	School	Experts, community, world, web
Student Autonomy	Teacher-defined; tightly managed	Co-defined and managed
Technology	Create the product	Manage the process

bie.org

SOURCES OF INSPIRATION
- ○ **Your Community**
- ○ **Current Events**
- ○ **Real-World Problem**
- ○ **Your Content Standards**
- ○ **Your File Cabinet**
- ○ **Your Colleagues**
- ○ **Your Students**
- ○ **Online Project Libraries**
- ○ **Project Search @ bie.org**
- ○ **PBLU.org**

bie.org

WHAT WILL MY STUDENTS/TEAMS CREATE?

	PRODUCT	
FOCUS	Same product, same focus *Presentation, water quality in our region*	Different product, same focus *Presentation/ photo essay, water quality in our region*
	Same product, different focus *Presentation, water quality in various parts of our region*	Different product, different focus *Presentation/ photo essay, water quality in various parts of our region*

bie.org

A DRIVING QUESTION...

FOR STUDENTS	FOR TEACHERS
Guides Project Work	Guides Planning & Reframes Content Standards or Big Ideas
Creates Interest and/or the Feeling of Challenge	Captures & Communicates the Purpose of the Project
Reminds Them "Why we're doing this today"	Initiates and Focuses Inquiry

bie.org

CHARRETTE PROTOCOL	TIME
PRESENTATION Presenter presents their project idea and DQ to a partner. The partner listens.	3 min
FRAMING QUESTION Presenter asks a specific question to frame the feedback. e.g. "What can I make better about…?" "How can I improve…?"	1 min
FEEDBACK Partner gives suggestions. Presenter listens. *Make sure your feedback is helpful, specific, and kind.*	2 min
OPEN DISCUSSION Presenter and partner have a dialogue about the suggestions/ feedback.	2 min
TOTAL	**8 min**

bie.org

Day 1 Lesson: Designing Projects

» What makes a project meaningful and effective?
» How do I get ideas for projects?
» What's a "Driving" Question?

Keywords	Notes

Questions & Ideas

Day 1 Lesson: Designing Projects, *continued*

Keywords

Notes

Questions & Ideas

TASK 1.2 Essential Elements Poster

Capture key ideas from the group presentations on the 8 Essential Elements of PBL. These may include the definition, examples of the element in action, or why this element is important.

Significant Content	21st Century Competencies
Driving Question	**Need to Know**

Essential Elements Poster, *continued*

In-Depth Inquiry	Critique and Revision
Voice and Choice	**Public Audience**

Small Acts of Courage

TASK 1.3 Project Search (optional)

Find TWO projects that might be of interest to you. Record notes below and be prepared to explain the projects to others.

Plan A: If you have a computer with Internet access, use the Project Search feature at **bie.org**.

Plan B: If you do not have Internet access, but have one of the books from BIE's *PBL Toolkit* series, look for ideas to adapt or expand upon on the following pages:

　　PBL Starter Kit: 9-28, 31-34, 41-42

　　PBL in the Elementary Grades: 3-5, 21-25, 39-41, 59-62, 153-183

Project #1	
Project Name & Source	*Resilience Cafe*
Project Idea	
General Content	
Driving Question (*if given*)	What can we learn from other people's inspiring stories of resilience that we might be able to use in our own lives?
Major Products	

Project #2	
Project Name & Source	A Day in the Life ... 7.W.3.3
Project Idea	Students learn how they are able ...
General Content	
Driving Question (*if given*)	
Major Products	

TASK 1.4 Getting Started

Part A. Select Significant Content for Your Project

List the general topics you plan to teach for the semester or year and then circle the content that jumps out as potential starting points for project ideas. Think about which standards — including the Common Core State Standards, if you use them — are the most important in the academic content areas you teach.

Content Areas & General Topics	Standards & Other Goals

Use the following rubric to do a self-check of Significant Content.

Significant Content	
Incorporates Best PBL Practices	■ The project is focused on teaching students important knowledge and skills derived from standards and key concepts at the heart of academic subject areas.
Needs Further Development	■ The project is aligned with standards and concepts from academic subject areas, but it may focus on too few, too many, or less important ones.
Lacks Essential Features of Effective PBL	■ The project is not aligned with standards and what students learn is not important in terms of concepts from academic subject areas.

Part B. Develop a Project Idea

Use the rubric below to guide you in developing two "main course" project ideas that involve In-Depth Inquiry.

Project Idea #1:

Project Idea #2:

Use the following rubric to do a self-check of In-Depth Inquiry.

In-Depth Inquiry	
Incorporates Best PBL Practices	▪ Inquiry is sustained and academically rigorous: students pose questions, gather & interpret data, ask further questions, and develop & evaluate solutions or build evidence for answers.
Needs Further Development	▪ Inquiry is superficial (information-gathering is the main task). ▪ Inquiry focuses on only one too-narrow topic, OR it tries to include too many issues, side topics, or tasks.
Lacks Essential Features of Effective PBL	▪ The "project" is more like an activity or applied learning task, rather than an extended inquiry. ▪ The "project" is unfocused, more like a unit with several tasks than one project.

Part C. Decide on Major Student Products

Check which major student product(s) you plan to have in your project, or add more of your choice.

Written Products
- ☐ Research Report
- ☐ Letter
- ☐ Brochure
- ☐ Script
- ☐ Blog
- ☐ Editorial
- ☐ Book Review
- ☐ Training Manual
- ☐ Mathematical/Engineering Analysis
- ☐ Scientific Study/Experiment Report
- ☐ Field Guide

Presentation Products
- ☐ Speech
- ☐ Debate
- ☐ Oral Defense
- ☐ Live Newscast
- ☐ Panel Discussion
- ☐ Play
- ☐ Musical Piece or Dance
- ☐ Lesson
- ☐ Public Event
- ☐ Sales Pitch

Media & Tech Products
- ☐ Audio Recording
- ☐ Slideshow
- ☐ Drawing/Painting
- ☐ Graphic Design
- ☐ Collage/Scrapbook
- ☐ Photo Essay
- ☐ Video/Animation
- ☐ Website
- ☐ Computer Program/App
- ☐ Digital Story/Comic

Constructed Products
- ☐ Small Scale Model
- ☐ Consumer Product
- ☐ Device/Machine
- ☐ Vehicle
- ☐ Invention
- ☐ Scientific Instrument
- ☐ Museum Exhibit
- ☐ Structure
- ☐ Garden

Planning Products
- ☐ Proposal
- ☐ Business Plan
- ☐ Design
- ☐ Bid
- ☐ Estimate
- ☐ Blueprint
- ☐ Timeline
- ☐ Flow Chart

Other:
....
....
....
....
....
....
....

Which products will be created by individuals?

....
....
....
....

Which products will be done as a team?

....
....
....
....

Part D. Involve a Public Audience

In some projects, the audience is the intended user of a product, reader of a piece of writing, or viewer of a website, media, art, or performance. This audience can be involved at the beginning, middle or end of a project. If students make formal presentations, the audience could be invited guests such as other students, teachers, administrators or staff; parents and community members; experts; or people reached online. The audience may offer feedback, ask questions, and/or evaluate students. Check the rubric for further guidance.

Use the space below to record notes about the Public Audience for your project and how you intend to involve them.

Use the following rubric to do a self-check of your Public Audience.

Public Audience	
Incorporates Best PBL Practices	▪ Students present or exhibit their work to an audience that includes other people from within and/or outside the school, which may include online audiences. ▪ Students present culminating products and defend them in detail & in depth (by explaining their reasoning behind choices they made, their inquiry process, etc).
Needs Further Development	▪ The audience for student presentations is limited to classmates & the teacher. ▪ Students present culminating products, but their explanation of how & why they did things is limited to a short, superficial question/answer session.
Lacks Essential Features of Effective PBL	▪ Students do not present or exhibit their work to an audience.

TASK 1.5 Writing a Driving Question

An effective Driving Question meets the following criteria:

1. Engaging for Students

- It interests students of the project's intended age, demographic background, community, etc.

- Students can understand the Question

- It does not sound like it came from a teacher or textbook

- It actively guides students through the project; it is not just a theme for the unit

- When applicable, it uses the words "I," "we," or "us" — not "you" or "students"

- It provokes students to ask further questions, beginning the inquiry process

- It might have a local context and/or a charge to take action, making it even more engaging — focusing on community issues and needs, or topics relevant to students' lives

2. Open-Ended

- It has several possible "right answers"

- The answer will be unique; it is not "Google-able" by students

- The answer is complex and leads to an in-depth inquiry

- It may be a "yes" or "no" question, but if so, the answer must require a detailed explanation or justification

3. Aligned with Learning Goals

- Students will need to learn important content and skills in order to create project products that answer the DQ

- It is not too big, requiring more knowledge than can be learned in a reasonable amount of time

- It does not necessarily state the learning goals explicitly — they can be specified later, when telling students more details about the project and the products to be created

Different Types of Driving Questions

A Philosophical or Debatable Issue, or an Intriguing Topic

- Who is a hero?

- When is war justified?

- What is a healthy community?

- Is our water safe to drink?

- How did the human species evolve?

- Why don't I fall off my skateboard?

- Why did European explorers of the New World risk their lives?

- Does Kashmir rightfully belong to Pakistan or India?

- Can DNA evidence be trusted in criminal trials?

- Should a park, an apartment building, or something else occupy the empty land in our community?

Specifying a Product, Task, or Problem to be Solved

- How can we create a picture book about the life cycle of animals in Oldham County?

- How can we create a web page for other kids that recommends some good books to read?

- How can we invent a new type of artificial log for a fireplace that burns with colorful flames but is environmentally friendly?

- How can we write a historically accurate story about a person who lived in our community long ago?

- How can we develop a business plan that will attract investors?

- How can we invent a new toy that is safe, not too expensive, and fun for four year olds?

- How can we design a theatre of a given size so it holds the maximum number of seats?

Adding a Real-World Role for Students

- How can we, as tour guides, plan a tour to show visitors what to see and do in our city?

- How can we, as structural engineers, design and test bridge models for a walkway over the river?

- How can we, as financial planners, advise a client about the best ways to invest and save money?

- How can we, as English town elders, decide who will board the ship to the New World and what they should take, so they can be successful colonists?

- How can we, as agricultural research scientists, design an experiment to show the Vice President of Marketing which company's bean seeds grow the fastest?

- How can we, as highway engineers, make a presentation to our boss about where to build a new highway in our region so that it does not harm animal habitats?

Part A. DQ Brainstorm

Brainstorm possible Driving Questions. Be sure to follow the guidelines listed below:

- Record as many options as you can, trying different formats and styles.

- Do not stop to discuss, judge, or answer questions.

- Write down every question exactly as it is stated the first time.

#1: How have certain events in my life made me who I am today

How has my

#2: How am I alike and how am I different from students in other parts of the world?

Part B. Determine Your Driving Question

Choose one or both of your Project Ideas, and write a draft Driving Question for it. You may refine your Driving Question later, after the Charrette, Gallery Walk, or whenever you wish.

Driving Question #1	
Draft	
Refined	

Driving Question #2	
Draft	
Refined	

Use the following rubric to do a self-check of your Driving Questions.

Driving Question	
Incorporates Best PBL Practices	■ The DQ captures the project's main focus. ■ The DQ is open-ended; it will allow students to develop more than one reasonable, complex answer. ■ The DQ is understandable & inspiring to students. ■ To answer the DQ, students will need to gain the intended knowledge, skills, & understanding.
Needs Further Development	■ The DQ relates to the project but does not capture its main focus; it may be more like a theme. ■ The DQ meets some criteria for an effective DQ, but lacks others (it may not be student-friendly; it may lead students toward one particular answer; it may be hard to answer thoroughly with the resources & time available and/or by students in this class).

Lacks Essential Features of Effective PBL	■ There is no DQ.
	■ The DQ is seriously flawed; for example:
	  ▶ It has a single or simple answer.
	  ▶ It is not engaging to students (it sounds too "academic," like it came from a textbook or appeals only to a teacher).

Pocket Guide to Probing Questions

For teachers and others who use feedback/critique protocols, it is important to understand the distinction between clarifying questions and probing questions — and the distinction between probing questions and recommendations for action.

Clarifying Questions are simple questions of fact. They have brief, factual answers and are meant to *provide needed information to member(s) of the audience*, not the presenter.

> **Some examples of clarifying questions:**
> - How much time does the project take?
> - How were the students teamed?
> - What resources did the students have available for this project?

Probing Questions are intended to *help the presenter* think more deeply about the issue at hand. This is not the time for a question that is really just a recommendation. If you can't come up with a probing question of your own, here are some question stems to get you started:

> **(Possible) Probing Question Stems:**
> - What sort of an impact do you think...?
> - What criteria did you use to...?
> - How did you decide/determine/conclude...?
> - What was your intention when...?
> - What would it look like if students...?
> - What are you hoping your students already know about...?
> - What is the connection between... and...?

> **Examples of Probing Questions About a Project**
> (Based on criteria for In-Depth Inquiry and Driving Question)
> - What criteria did you use to develop your project idea/DQ so that it engages students?
>   *(Engaging for Students)*
> - When students answer your DQ, how will you ensure the answers are unique?
>   *(Open-Ended)*
> - What are you hoping your students already know about the topic of water pollution?
>   *(Aligned with Learning Goals)*
> - Why do you think your topic is too narrow (or broad)?
>   *(Project Idea; In-Depth Inquiry)*
> - What is the connection between the product and student inquiry? Will they have the opportunity for ongoing, extended inquiry through the development of that product?
>   *(Project Idea; In-Depth Inquiry)*

Adapted from National School Reform Faculty (2002) by the Buck Institute for Education (2014). Developed by Gene Thompson-Grove, Edorah Frazer, Faith Dunne; includes work by Charlotte Danielson.

Day 2:
ASSESSING PROJECTS

The following tasks are to be completed today:

- **TASK 2.1 High Quality Assessment**

- **TASK 2.2 Assessment Planning** (optional)

- **TASK 2.3 Differentiation Time**

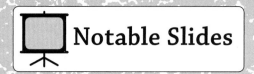

Notable Slides

GALLERY WALK	TIME
SET-UP Hang posters and distribute sticky notes.	3 min
ROLE ASSIGNMENT (OPTIONAL) Provide feedback on the following areas: • Significant Content – Is the amount of content appropriate for this project? • Driving Question – Is the DQ engaging, grade-level appropriate? • Student Products & Public Audience – Are the designated products and the public audience an authentic fit for the content?	2 min
GALLERY WALK & FEEDBACK Silently record feedback on sticky notes. Offer one or more of the following: • "Praise" – Tell why you like it; why it is a strength • "Question" – Ask questions about pieces of the plan that are unclear • "Polish" – Provide suggestions for improvement *Make sure your feedback is helpful, specific, and kind.*	20 min
REFLECTION In your journal, reflect on the feedback and discuss the Gallery Walk.	5 min
TOTAL	**30 min**

bie.org

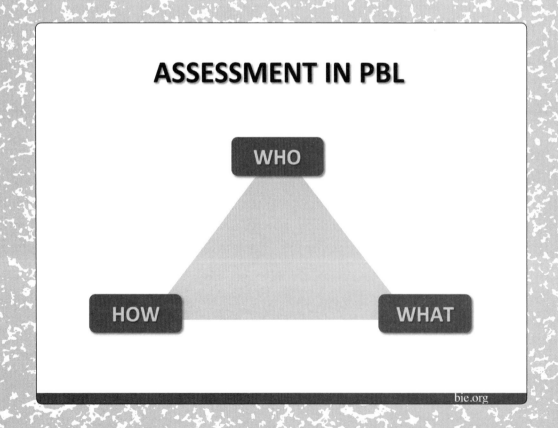

bie.org

Day 2 Lesson: Assessing Projects

How do I assess student learning in a project?

Keywords	Notes

Questions & Ideas

Keywords

Notes

Questions & Ideas

TASK 2.1 High Quality Assessment

Before planning the assessments for your project, it is important to consider what high quality assessment is. On the y-chart below, record descriptors for the following:

- What high quality assessment looks like (e.g., examples of assessment; actions students take when completing a high quality assessment)

- What high quality assessment feels like (e.g., student affect; teacher experience)

- What high quality assessment sounds like (e.g., what language would you hear students use; what is the tone of conversations about high quality assessment)

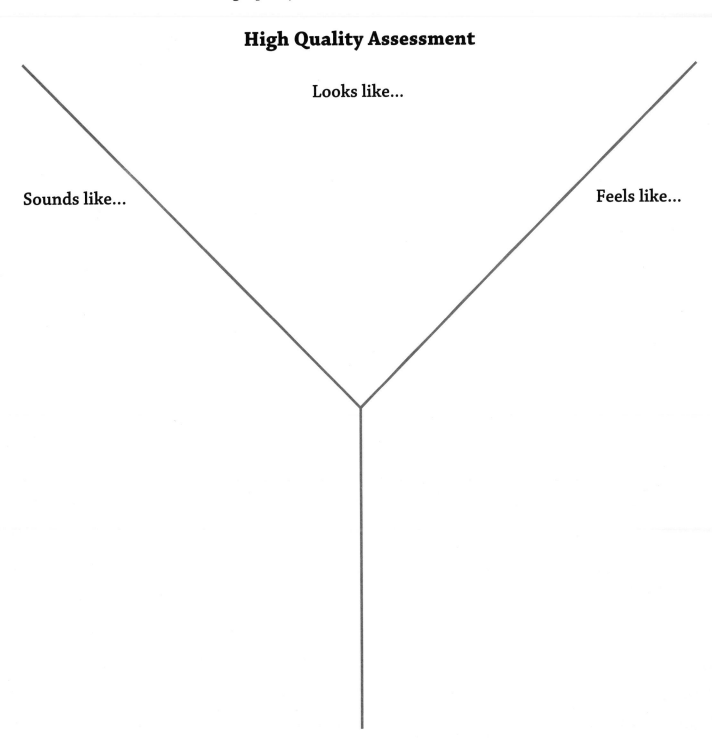

High Quality Assessment

Looks like...

Sounds like...

Feels like...

TASK 2.2 Assessment Planning

For each major product listed in **Task 1.4 Part C**, think of the formative products you will check along the way to make sure students are on the right track. Use the Project Assessment Maps on the next page to record your plans, following these steps:

1. On the far left line of the map, write the major product (a summative assessment).

2. In the center of the map, write significant content and a 21st century competency that students will need to learn in order to create the major product.

3. Once you have determined *what* you will need to formatively assess, decide *which* formative products or processes you will use to check for understanding and quality of work. Write these on the lines on the right.

Example:

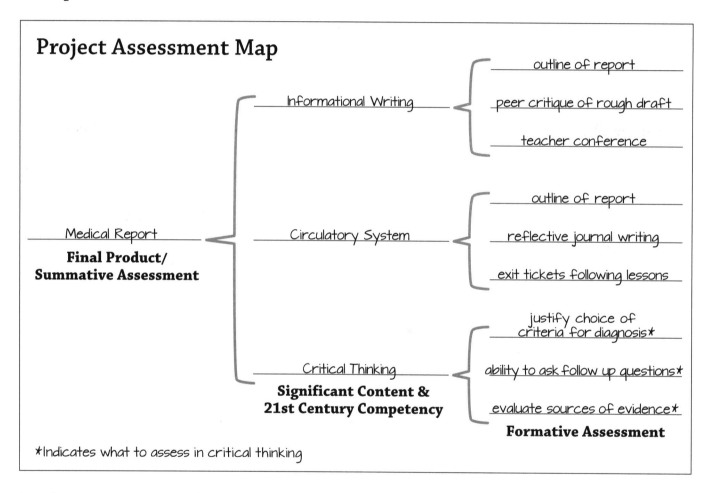

Use the Project Design: Student Learning Guide on the following pages and the extra copy in *Resources* to help you scaffold the content and skills students will need to complete major products and performances.

Project Assessment Map

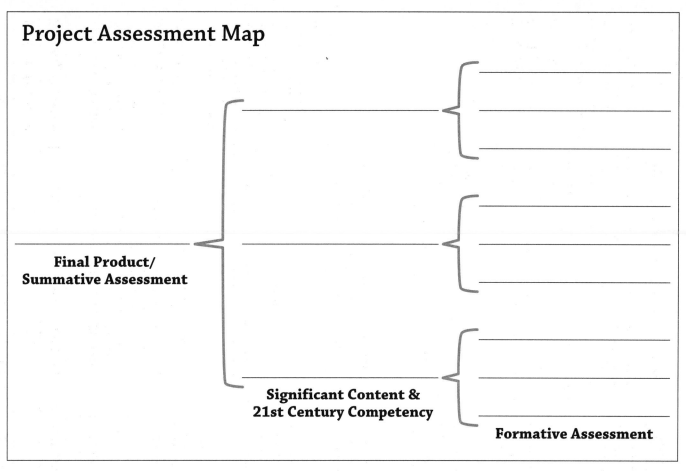

Final Product/
Summative Assessment

Significant Content &
21st Century Competency

Formative Assessment

Project Assessment Map

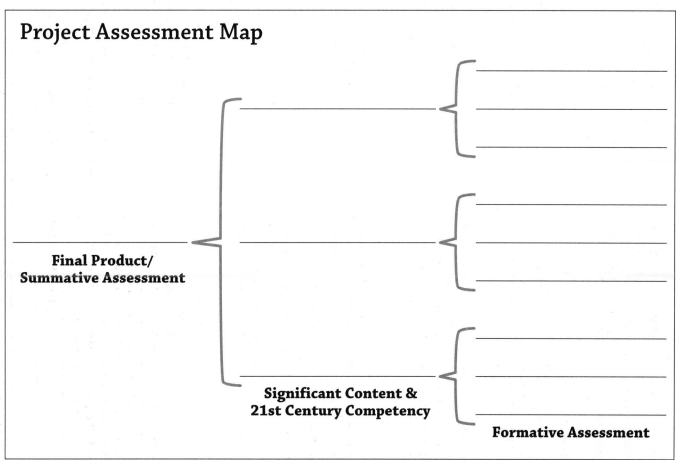

Final Product/
Summative Assessment

Significant Content &
21st Century Competency

Formative Assessment

Project: Medical Interns

Driving Question: How can we, as medical interns, recommend the best treatment for a sick patient?

Final Product(s) Presentations, Performances, Products and/or Services	Learning Outcomes/Targets content & 21st century competencies needed by students to successfully complete products	Checkpoints/Formative Assessments to check for learning and ensure students are on track	Instructional Strategies for All Learners provided by teacher, other staff, experts; includes scaffolds, materials, lessons aligned to learning outcomes and formative assessments
Medical Report (individual) Anchor learning target: I can conduct short research projects using several sources to diagnose and treat a sick patient. (W.5.7 - Research to Build and Present Knowledge)	I can identify the parts of the circulatory system. (Life Sciences - Circulatory system)	1. Summary of resources 2. Exit tickets following lessons 3. Lab notes/science journal 4. Quiz	• Teacher model of summary writing/note taking • Science labs on circulation • Interview with MD • Textbook lesson; video
	I can write a report to inform a patient of his/her diagnosis. (Writing 5.4 - Informational text writing)	1. Outline of report 2. Reflective journal writing 3. Drafts of report (peer/teacher feedback) 4. Charrette	• Examination of exemplar papers to determine structure, teacher model • Interview with MD • Writer's workshop, fishbowl modeling of peer critique • Review probing questions; model of charrette
	I can explain my diagnosis using evidence with facts, details, and quotations. (Writing 5.2.b - Informational text writing)	1. Summary of resources 2. Drafts of report (peer/teacher feedback) 3. Teacher conference	• Teacher model of summary writing/note taking • Writer's workshop (differentiate for gifted/struggling writers)
	I can summarize or paraphrase information from my research. (Writing 5.8 - Research to Build and Present Knowledge)	1. Summary of resources 2. Quick write assessment 3. Summary sentences on exit tickets	• Teacher model of summary writing/note taking • Writer's workshop (differentiate for gifted/struggling writers) • Small group activity on summary sentences (with EL students)
Diagnosis Presentation (team) Anchor learning target: I can report on a topic in a logical way using details to support my ideas. (SL. 5.4)	I can use visual aids to enhance the content and message of my presentation.	1. Draft of visual aids (peer/teacher feedback) 2. Fishbowl 3. Charrette	• Examination of exemplar visual aids; watch a student presentation w/ visual aids on video
	I can respond to audience questions accurately and clearly. (Presentation Skills - Speaking and Listening 5.5)		• Questioning techniques lesson w/ partner practice; interview with MD • Review probing questions; model of charrette
	I can evaluate multiple sources on my topic and integrate valid sources into my presentation to speak knowledgeably about the topic. (Critical Thinking/Reading Informational Text 5.7)	1. Summary of resources 2. Outline of report 3. Charrette 4. Practice Presentation (peer/teacher feedback)	• Internet search lesson on finding valid sources; small group support • Align evidence and claims in teams; examine exemplar papers • Review probing questions; model of charrette

PROJECT DESIGN: STUDENT LEARNING GUIDE

Project:

Driving Question:

Final Product(s) Presentations, Performances, Products and/or Services	Learning Outcomes/Targets content & 21st century competencies needed by students to successfully complete products	Checkpoints/Formative Assessments to check for learning and ensure students are on track	Instructional Strategies for All Learners provided by teacher, other staff, experts; includes scaffolds, materials, lessons aligned to learning outcomes and formative assessments
(individual **and** team)			

PROJECT DESIGN: STUDENT LEARNING GUIDE

Project:

Driving Question:

Final Product(s) Presentations, Performances, Products and/or Services (individual **and** team)	Learning Outcomes/Targets content & 21st century competencies needed by students to successfully complete products	Checkpoints/Formative Assessments to check for learning and ensure students are on track	Instructional Strategies for All Learners provided by teacher, other staff, experts; includes scaffolds, materials, lessons aligned to learning outcomes and formative assessments

TASK 2.3 Differentiation Time

Use the space below to record your notes and new understandings as you move through the activities.

Differentiation Time, *continued*

Day 3:
MANAGING PROJECTS

The following tasks are to be completed today:

- TASK 3.1 Entry Event Planning

- TASK 3.2 Project Presentation

- TASK 3.3 Collective Wisdom

- TASK 3.4 Forming Teams (optional)

- TASK 3.5 Über Meta-Moment

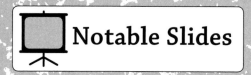 Notable Slides

EXAMPLE ENTRY EVENTS
○ Field Trip
○ Guest Speaker
○ Film, Video, Website
○ Simulation or Activity
○ Provocative Reading
○ Startling Statistics
○ Puzzling Problem
○ Piece of Real or Mock Correspondence
○ Song, Poem, Art
○ Lively Discussion

bie.org

CRITICAL FRIENDS PROTOCOL	TIME
PRESENTATION Presenters explain their project; Audience listens.	5 min
CLARIFICATION Audience asks short clarifying questions; Presenters respond.	2 min
ASSESSMENT Audience quietly uses Project Design Rubric to assess the project; Presenters wait.	1 min
"I LIKE…" Audience shares what they liked (Best Practices); Presenters listen.	3 min
"I WONDER…" Audience shares concerns (Lacks Features or Needs Development); Presenters listen.	3 min
REFLECTION Presenters reflect on useful feedback; Audience listens.	3 min
"I HAVE…" Audience shares ideas & resources for the project; Presenters may respond.	3 min
TOTAL	**20 min**

bie.org

"FIRSTDAYS"

Entry Event

Driving Question

Final products

Start Need to Know list

Project teams formed

Discussion of expectations for teamwork

First team meeting: team-building activity, contract, initial task list

bie.org

PROJECT DOCUMENTS
○ **Project Info Sheet**
○ **Project Calendar**
○ **Rubric(s)**
○ **Checklist of Requirements**
○ **Points/Percentages for Grading**
○ **Templates for Contracts, Task Lists, Action Plans, etc.**
○ **Team Roster**
○ **Presentation Day Schedule**
○ **Resource List**

bie.org

PROJECT WALL
○ **Driving Question**
○ **Need to Know List of Questions**
○ **Word/Concept List**
○ **Project Calendar**
○ **Rubric(s)**
○ **Sample products**

bie.org

#pbl @biepbl

twitter.com/biepbl

pblu.org

youtube.com/biepbl

plus.google.com/+BIEPBL

pinterest.com/biepbl/

facebook.com/biepbl

bie.org

Day 3 Lesson: Managing Projects

How do I manage a project?

Keywords	Notes

Questions & Ideas

Day 3 Lesson: Managing Projects, *continued*

Keywords

Notes

Questions & Ideas

TASK 3.1 Entry Event Planning

An Entry Event has two major purposes: to spark student interest and curiosity, and to begin the inquiry process by leading students to ask questions.

Use the space below to record notes about the Entry Event for your project and how this creates an authentic Need to Know for students.

Need to Know	
Incorporates Best PBL Practices	▪ The project motivates students to learn new content knowledge or gain skills because they genuinely find the project's topic, Driving Question, and tasks to be relevant and meaningful. ▪ The Entry Event will powerfully engage students, both emotionally & intellectually (make them feel invested in the project & provoke inquiry)
Needs Further Development	▪ The project motivates students to learn new content knowledge or gain skills because they see the need for them in order to complete project products and not be embarrassed to present their work. ▪ The Entry Event will gain student attention but it will not begin the inquiry process by creating a need to know or generate questions about the topic of the project.
Lacks Essential Features of Effective PBL	▪ The project does not motivate students to learn new content knowledge or gain skills. ▪ No Entry Event is planned. Day one of the project will feel like any other day (or worse, because it seems like more work than usual).

TASK 3.2 Project Presentation

In the Critical Friends Protocol, you will be explaining how your project meets the 8 Essential Elements of PBL, and your colleagues will give you feedback. Begin by stating the grade level and subject area, project title and idea, and the major student products. Tell your listeners if you would especially like feedback on any particular issue. Record notes about the questions below to help plan your presentation.

1. Significant Content: What CCSS, other standards, or important learning goals are you teaching and assessing through this project?

- Cite textual evidence to support inferences; compare & contrast fictional portrayal of historical time/event w/ actual time/event; write narrative compositions using elements of short story or poetry

2. 21st Century Competencies: Which of the "4 C's" or other competencies will you *teach* and *assess*?

- collaboration
- creativity

3. In-Depth Inquiry: How will students engage in questioning and investigation?

- students research an historical figure, interview a community member & reflect on themselves to find common qualities of resilience; they have to synthesize all of these areas to create their short story/poem

4. Driving Question: What overall question will focus your project?

What can we learn from other people's stories of resilience?

5. Need to Know: How will your Entry Event and project launch lead students to ask questions and motivate them to learn?

The entry events of having a community member come in & tell a story as well as research during the project will motivate students & lead them to ask ?s.

6. Voice & Choice: What opportunities will students have to make decisions about the project's product(s) or process?

Can choose historical figure, community person, poem or short story & multi-media design

7. Critique & Revision: What processes will you include for students to engage in critique, with time for revising their ideas and products or to conduct further inquiry?

students will have their writing peer & teacher reviewed; their "Spoken Word" presentations will be reviewed and practiced 3 times

8. Public Audience: With whom will students share their work, beyond their classmates and teacher?

With their chosen community member and any family member who wants to come with them; the comm. member also open invitation to all members of the retirement community (held @ Timbercrest Assembly Room).

Note-Taking Guide for Critical Friends Protocol

Use the space below to note feedback you would give to the project presenter(s).
Refer to the criteria described in the Project Design Rubric.

5th gr

"I like…"
(Strengths of the project; how it **Incorporates Best PBL Practices**, as described in the 3rd column of the Rubric)

_____
_____
_____
_____
_____
_____

"I wonder…"
(Potential weaknesses of the project; how it **Lacks Essential Features of Effective PBL** or **Needs Further Development**, as described in the 1st or 2nd columns of the Rubric)

(look @ other museums)
_____
_____
_____
_____
_____

"I have…"
(Ideas you have that might enhance the project; resources, materials, or other suggestions)

_____
_____
_____
_____
_____
_____

Note-Taking Guide for Critical Friends Protocol

Use the space below to note feedback you would give to the project presenter(s).
Refer to the criteria described in the Project Design Rubric.

"I like..."
(Strengths of the project; how it **Incorporates Best PBL Practices**, as described in the 3rd column of the Rubric)

"I wonder..."
(Potential weaknesses of the project; how it **Lacks Essential Features of Effective PBL** or **Needs Further Development**, as described in the 1st or 2nd columns of the Rubric)

"I have..."
(Ideas you have that might enhance the project; resources, materials, or other suggestions)

Note-Taking Guide for Critical Friends Protocol

Use the space below to note feedback you would give to the project presenter(s).
Refer to the criteria described in the Project Design Rubric.

"I like..."
(Strengths of the project; how it **Incorporates Best PBL Practices**, as described in the 3rd column
of the Rubric)

"I wonder..."
(Potential weaknesses of the project; how it **Lacks Essential Features of Effective PBL** or **Needs Further
Development**, as described in the 1st or 2nd columns of the Rubric)

"I have..."
(Ideas you have that might enhance the project; resources, materials, or other suggestions)

TASK 3.3 Collective Wisdom

It is impossible to have a solution to every management challenge in your back pocket. However, as you experienced today in the Collective Wisdom activity, the wisdom is often in the room. Take a moment to return to the management challenges you might face in your project. What strategies or ideas resonated with you?

Use the space to record notes about strategies you would like to try in your classroom.

*+ = pairing w/ T.C. resident - bringing ages together
+ good for T.C. residents
+ good to use both fiction + nonfiction
+ guest speaker as entry event
+ option of short story or poem
+ present @ T.C. &good for both ages
+ subject matter - resilience - human side to
          history*

Wonder
 *- comparison of fiction - how do - could
          leave out
 - pair kids w/ T.C. ? Nancy Sare -
          some kids will all ready be paired
          w/ some residents
 - students generate interview ?'s
 - bring in other ages ?
          ⇨ yes - T.C. only for
 - show stories of kids their age -
          girl who lost arm to Shark
 - logistics of getting kids to T.C.
 - contact girls in parasailing accident in
          (Hgn)   Florida)*

Panel of people for

TASK 3.4 Forming Teams

As you are forming "The Kids" on the following pages into project teams, think about and be ready to discuss:

- What criteria did you use to form the teams? Are there circumstances when this would be different?

- What are some issues or considerations that arise when forming teams?

- What about letting students choose their own teams, or at least having input? Is that a good idea, and how might that be managed?

Use the space below to record notes on the above:

TASK 3.5 Über Meta-Moment

PBL is about managing more than just the process; it is about managing student learning. Reflect on your experience as a learner in the PBL 101 Workshop. What scaffolds, instructional strategies, groupings, and processes were used throughout the workshop to manage learning and promote success? How did they support your understanding of the 8 Essential Elements of PBL and completion of your project design?

"What"
(What have you learned or experienced?)

"So What"
(Why does this strategy or scaffold matter?)

"Now What"
(How might you use that strategy when you return to your classroom?

S. BEAUTY

Skill	Rating
Acad. Ability	H
Leadership	M
Behavior	M
Art Skills	L
Tech Skills	H

Notes: popular; tends to drift off

C. NDERELLA

Skill	Rating
Acad. Ability	M
Leadership	M
Behavior	M
Art Skills	H
Tech Skills	L

Notes: was home schooled; works hard, but always loses homework

M. HATTER

Skill	Rating
Acad. Ability	H
Leadership	H
Behavior	M
Art Skills	L
Tech Skills	M

Notes: ADD; creative, but sometimes off topic

W. POOH

Skill	Rating
Acad. Ability	M
Leadership	L
Behavior	L
Art Skills	H
Tech Skills	L

Notes: kind; friendly; is honey-goal-oriented

A. LICE

Skill	Rating
Acad. Ability	H
Leadership	H
Behavior	H
Art Skills	M
Tech Skills	M

Notes: curious; imaginative; strong-willed; has good head on shoulders

B. AMBI

Skill	Rating
Acad. Ability	M
Leadership	L
Behavior	M
Art Skills	M
Tech Skills	L

Notes: cooperative; emotionally fragile

P. PAN

Skill	Rating
Acad. Ability	M
Leadership	L
Behavior	L
Art Skills	M
Tech Skills	M

Notes: immature; active; well-liked; may distract others

M. ULAN

Skill	Rating
Acad. Ability	L
Leadership	H
Behavior	?
Art Skills	H
Tech Skills	M

Notes: EL, assertive; recent immigrant

P. CAHONTAS

Skill	Rating
Acad. Ability	M
Leadership	H
Behavior	H
Art Skills	H
Tech Skills	L

Notes: EL Level 4; helpful; cross-cultural

T. NKERBELL

Skill	Rating
Acad. Ability	L
Leadership	M
Behavior	L
Art Skills	M
Tech Skills	H

Notes: EL; ADD; needs attention and praise; puts glitter on everything

S. WHITE

Skill	Rating
Acad. Ability	H
Leadership	M
Behavior	M
Art Skills	H
Tech Skills	L

Notes: works well with others, especially teams of 8

E. QUEEN

Skill	Rating
Acad. Ability	H
Leadership	H
Behavior	M
Art Skills	M
Tech Skills	H

Notes: strong leader; a bit of a mean girl; prefers Apple to PC

P. CHARMING

Category	Rating
Acad. Ability	M
Leadership	M
Behavior	M
Art Skills	L
Tech Skills	L

Notes: athletic; confident; popular

S. NEEZY

Category	Rating
Acad. Ability	M
Leadership	M
Behavior	H
Art Skills	M
Tech Skills	L

Notes: cooperative, but misses school sometimes due to illness

G. RUMPY

Category	Rating
Acad. Ability	H
Leadership	H
Behavior	M
Art Skills	L
Tech Skills	M

Notes: anger issues; controlling; likes to keep things organized

D. OC

Category	Rating
Acad. Ability	H
Leadership	H
Behavior	H
Art Skills	M
Tech Skills	M

Notes: intelligent; bit of a know-it-all

B. ASHFUL

Category	Rating
Acad. Ability	M
Leadership	M
Behavior	M
Art Skills	H
Tech Skills	H

Notes: Gifted?; shy but excellent drawing skills

S. LEEPY

Category	Rating
Acad. Ability	M
Leadership	L
Behavior	M
Art Skills	M
Tech Skills	H

Notes: Sp Ed; sometimes loses focus; skips breakfast?

H. APPY

Category	Rating
Acad. Ability	L
Leadership	M
Behavior	H
Art Skills	H
Tech Skills	M

Notes: team player; good attitude; medicated?

L. MERMAID

Category	Rating
Acad. Ability	H
Leadership	H
Behavior	M
Art Skills	M
Tech Skills	L

Notes: sets high goals; athletic; Sp Ed (speech impaired)

B. EAST

Category	Rating
Acad. Ability	H
Leadership	L
Behavior	M
Art Skills	L
Tech Skills	M

Notes: loner; easily frustrated; has hidden potential?

G. PETTO

Category	Rating
Acad. Ability	M
Leadership	H
Behavior	M
Art Skills	H
Tech Skills	H

Notes: EL (Italian); mature; handy

P. NOCCHIO

Category	Rating
Acad. Ability	L
Leadership	L
Behavior	L
Art Skills	M
Tech Skills	L

Notes: EL (Italian); willing to follow others, but with strings attached; lies

J. CRICKET

Category	Rating
Acad. Ability	H
Leadership	H
Behavior	H
Art Skills	M
Tech Skills	H

Notes: Ivy League bound; competent; ethical; chirpy; small

RESOURCES

8 Essentials for Project-Based Learning

Some "projects" border on busywork. Others involve meaningful inquiry that engages students' minds.

John Larmer
John R. Mergendoller, PhD.
Buck Institute for Education

As Mrs. McIntyre walked around the high school science classroom, she plopped a packet of papers on each student's desk and announced a "project." Each student would create a poster about a water-borne bacterium that can be harmful to humans, the bacterium's effects, and disease prevention and treatment. The handouts included an assignment sheet with due dates and grading policy, a rubric, a guide for designing the poster, and a list of websites and books. The teacher would display the best posters.

• • •

Students at Mare Island Technical Academy in Vallejo present their project work to an audience.

Sound familiar? When you were in school, did you make posters, dioramas, and models of buildings or volcanoes? If you are a teacher, have you asked students to research a topic and present information with PowerPoint slides? These are all-too-common examples of the kind of meaning-lite assignments that teachers bill as projects. A classroom filled with student posters may suggest that students have been engaged in meaningful learning. But it is the process of students' learning and the depth of their cognitive engagement – rather than the resulting product – that distinguishes projects from busywork.

What Every Good Project Needs

A project is meaningful if it fulfills two criteria. First, students must perceive it as personally meaningful, as a task that matters and that they want to do well. Second, a meaningful project fulfills an educational purpose. Well-designed and well-implemented Project Based Learning (PBL) is meaningful in both ways.

As educators with the Buck Institute for Education, we provide professional development to help schools set up a sustained program of in-depth Project Based Learning throughout a district, network, or state. In our work with teachers, we have identified eight essential elements of meaningful projects. Let's look at each element by considering what the fictional Mrs. McIntyre could have done to create a meaningful project instead of handing out prepared packets.

1. Significant content

Back when she began planning the project, Ms. McIntyre started with her content standards. She knew the standards about microorganisms and disease were reflected in high number of items on her state's test, and her own judgment told her this was an important topic for young people to understand. She also thought her students would find the topic significant, since bacteria and disease had concrete effects on their lives.

• • •

Project Based Learning is sometimes mistakenly believed, based on old stereotypes, to be an ineffective vehicle for teaching content. But while is it is true that a teacher cannot "cover" (which isn't, after all, the same as "teach") as much material in a project as he or she could through lectures, worksheets, and textbooks, students in a well-designed project understand the content more deeply. Teachers should plan a project to focus on important knowledge and concepts derived from standards. The content should also reflect what the teacher thinks is essential to understand about the topic. And students should find the content to be significant in terms of their own lives and interests.

2. A Need to Know

Imagine that on the first day of the infectious disease unit, Ms. McIntyre showed a video depicting scenes of a beautiful beach, which ended with a shot of a sign saying, "Beach Closed: Contaminated Water." Suppose watching this video led to a lively (and sometimes disgusting) discussion in which students shared their experiences with suspicious water quality, discussing times when beaches had been closed and why. The teacher could then introduce the project by telling students that they would be learning more about ocean pollution and taking action to combat it.

• • •

Teachers can powerfully activate students' need to know content by launching a project with an "entry event" that engages student interest and initiates questioning. An entry event can be almost anything: a video, a lively discussion, a guest speaker, a field trip, or a piece of mock correspondence that sets up a scenario. In contrast, announcing a project with a packet of papers is likely to turn students off; it looks like a prelude to busywork.

Many students find school work meaningless because they don't perceive a need to know what they are being taught. They are unmotivated by a

teacher's suggestion that they should learn something because they'll need it later in life, or for the next course, or simply because "it's going to be on the test." With a compelling student project, the reason for learning relevant material becomes clear: I need to know this to meet the challenge I've accepted.

3. A Driving Question

After the discussion about beach pollution, Ms. McIntyre led students in brainstorming possible solutions, such as enacting laws, designing better waste-treatment systems, and raising public awareness about the need to reduce contaminants. Students created a Driving Question to focus their efforts, focusing on a specific, local area: How can we reduce the number of days Foster's beach is closed because of poor water quality?

A good driving question captures the heart of the project in clear, compelling language.

A good Driving Question captures the heart of the project in clear, compelling language, which gives students a sense of purpose and challenge. The Question should be provocative, open-ended, complex, and linked to the core of what you want students to learn. It could be abstract (When is war justified?); concrete (Is our water safe to drink?); or focused on solving a problem (How can we improve this website so that more young people will use it?).

A project without a Driving Question is like an essay without a thesis. Without a thesis statement, a reader might be able to pick out the main point a writer is trying to make; but with a thesis statement, the main point is unmistakable. Without a Driving Question, students may not understand why they are undertaking

Handwritten annotations at top: Life Skills → "21st Century Skills → Collaboration (#1) → communication → creativity → critical thinking

a project. They know that the series of assigned activities has some connection with a time period, a place, or concept. But if you asked, "What is the point of all these activities?" they might only be able to offer, "Because we're making a poster."

4. Student Voice and Choice
handwritten: 1. makes more meaningful

Once her students' interest was piqued by a challenging question, Ms. McIntyre explained the requirements for the "Don't Close the Beach" project, which included *handwritten: 2. ownership* an individually written paper, a product of the students' choice created by teams, and an oral presentation of their work accompanied by media technology. Students chose to develop media kits for journalists, video public service announcements, web pages, brochures, and letters to government and industry officials, among other products.

handwritten: requirements + elements of choice

This element of Project Based Learning is key. In terms of making a project feel meaningful to students, the more voice and choice, the better. However, teachers should design projects with the extent of student choice that fits their own style and students.

On the limited-choice end of the scale, learners can select what topic to study within a general Driving Question or choose how to design, create, and present products. As a middle ground, teachers might provide a limited menu of options for creative products to prevent students from becoming overwhelmed by choices. On the "the more the better" end of the scale, students can decide what product they will create, what resources they will use, and how they will structure their time. Students could even choose a project's topic and Driving Question.

5. 21st Century Competencies
Once Ms. McIntyre's students had decided on actions that would help them respond to the Driving Question, they got to work. Collaboration was central to the project. Students formed teams of three or four and began planning what tasks they would do and how they would work together.

As they worked, each team regularly paused to review how well they were collaborating and communicating, using rubrics the class had developed with the teacher. To boost collaboration skills, Mrs. McIntyre used role-playing and team-building activities. She showed students how to use time and task organizers. They practiced oral presentation skills and learned to produce videos and podcasts.

Students find project work more meaningful if they conduct real inquiry.

In writing journals, students reflected on their thinking and problem-solving processes, which they knew they would need to explain in their oral presentation.

• • •

A project should give students opportunities to build 21st century competencies such as critical thinking, collaboration, communication, and creativity/innovation, which will serve them well in the workplace and life. This exposure to authentic skills meets the second criterion for meaningful work – an important purpose. A teacher in a Project Based Learning environment explicitly teaches and assesses these skills and provides frequent opportunities for students to assess themselves.

6. In-Depth Inquiry
After the discussion about encounters with pollution, in addition to choosing a Driving Question, Ms. McIntyre's students as a whole class generated a list of more detailed questions about diseases, bacteria and their effects, and sources of water contamination. Questions included, What diseases can you get from water? Do you have to drink it to get sick? and Where do bacteria come from? The teams fine-tuned their questions and discussed how to find answers from their teacher, books, articles,

websites, experts, and visits to Foster's Beach.

As these learners found answers, they raised and investigated new questions. Students synthesized the information they gathered and used it both to inform their individually-written papers on the Driving Question and to help create their team's product related to that question.

• • •

Students find project work to be more meaningful if they are asked to conduct real inquiry – which does not mean finding information in books or websites and pasting it onto a poster. In real inquiry, students follow a trail that begins with their own questions, leads to a search for resources and the discovery of answers, and which ultimately leads to generating new questions, testing ideas, and drawing their own conclusions. With real inquiry comes innovation – a new answer to a Driving Question, a new product, a new solution to a problem. The teacher does not ask students to simply reproduce teacher- or textbook-provided information in a pretty format.

To guide students in real inquiry, refer students to the list of questions they generated after the entry event. Coach them to add to this list as they discover new insights. The classroom culture should value questioning, hypothesizing, and openness to new ideas and perspectives.

7. Critique and Revision
As they developed their ideas and products, student teams reviewed and critiqued one another's work, referring to rubrics and exemplars. Ms. McIntyre checked research notes, reviewed rough drafts and plans, and met with teams to monitor their progress.

• • •

Formalizing a process for critique and revision during a project makes learning meaningful because it emphasizes that creating high-quality products and performances is an important purpose of the endeavor. Students need to learn that most people's first attempts don't result in high quality and that revision is a frequent feature of real-world work.

In addition to providing direct feedback, a teacher should coach students in using rubrics or other sets of criteria to critique one another's work. Teachers can arrange for experts or adult mentors to provide feedback, which is especially meaningful to students because of the source.

8. Public Audience
In Ms. McIntyre's class, teams presented their analyses of water contamination issues and their proposals for addressing the problem at an exhibition night. The invited audience included parents, peers, and representatives of community, business, and government organizations.

Students answered questions and reflected on how they completed the project, next steps they might take, and what they gained in terms of knowledge and skills – and pride.

• • •

Schoolwork is more meaningful when it's not done only for the teacher or the test. When students present their work to a real audience, they care more about its quality. Once again, it's "the more, the better" when it comes to the authenticity. Students might replicate the kinds of tasks done by professionals – but even better, they might create real products that people outside school use.

Students at Tamalpais High School in California study U.S. History in a project.

The Rest of the Story
The hypothetical project described here was inspired by a real project, "Media Saves the Beach," carried out by students at High Tech High in San Diego, California. In this real-life project, students worked alongside established local groups to advocate cleaner shorelines. Several government agencies came through with funding for water monitoring at local beaches.

In truth, one of the products students created was a poster. What made that poster different from the meaning-lite one Ms. McIntyre had assigned? The High Tech High students chose to do their poster because it was an effective way to communicate their message at Exhibition Night – and the team stood nearby to explain it. To create the poster, students engaged in an extended process of inquiry, critique, and revision. They learned important things in the process. In short, even a poster can be meaning-heavy if it's part of a project embodying the eight essential elements of Project Based Learning.

Author's Note: Individuals and some place names in this article are pseudonyms.

John Larmer (415-883-0122; john larmer@bie.org) is director of product development and **John R. Mergendoller** (john@bie.org) is executive director at the Buck Institute for Education, 18 Commercial Blvd., Novato, CA 94949.

Buck Institute for Education
18 Commercial Blvd.
Novato, CA, USA 94949
ph: 415-883-0122
www.bie.org
youtube.com/biepbl
twitter.com/biepbl

Common Types of Projects*

* NOTE: These are meant to be good but not perfect examples of projects. How might you critique them?

1. Exploration of a Philosophical Question

Secondary Example:

Project Title: Old Enough To...?

Grade: 9

Project Idea: Students read *The Catcher in the Rye* and short stories whose themes are adolescence and growing up. They conduct interviews with people of various ages, survey their peers, then write their own reflections on the topic, which they publish on a class blog.

DQ: When do we grow up?

Content: (ELA) theme in literature (RL.9-10.2); narrative writing (RL.9-10.3); knowledge of language (L.9-10.3)

Major Products: Various literary analysis writing assignments; interview questions and edited responses; survey and analysis of results; blog posts

Public Audience: online readers of the class blog

Elementary Example:

Project Title: Pizza and the World of Work*

Grade: 2

Project Idea: Students interview adult family members and friends and visit local businesses to find out what it's like to work. They plan how to run a pizza restaurant in their classroom, gather ingredients and supplies, test recipes, create menus and advertisements, and operate it for two days.

DQ: What does it mean to work?

Content: (Math) measurement & data (MD.2.A.1-.4); addition & subtraction (NBT.2.B.5-.9); (Biological Science) types of plants; (Social Studies) community & economics; (ELA) reading informational text (RI.2.1-.2); informative writing (W.2.2; 2.5-.6)

Major Products: Journal; recipes, schedules, advertisements, menus, pizza

Public Audience: school staff, other students

*This project is described in more detail in BIE's book, *PBL in the Elementary Grades*

2. Investigation of a Historical Event, Time Period, or Natural Phenomenon

Secondary Examples:

Project Title: It's the Bomb

Grade: 10

Project Idea: Students act as advisors to President Harry Truman in July, 1945, who must recommend whether to drop the atomic bomb on Japan.

DQ: Should the U.S. drop the atomic bomb on Japan?

Content: (World History) World War II, European & Pacific theatres; (Science) atomic energy; (ELA) literacy in history/social science (RH.9-10.1-.6)

Major Products: Briefs describing the status of the war; oral presentation to the President and a panel of key decision-makers

Public Audience: guest adults will act as the President and his panel

---

Project Title: Evolve or Die!

Grade: 6

Project Idea: Students, in the role of scientists, make predictions about how various animals might evolve in response to changes in their local environment due to climate change. They create illustrated pages for the website of a state wildlife protection agency and present them to a representative of the agency.

DQ: How might animals evolve in a changing climate?

Content: (Biological Science) habitat, anatomical structures of animals; evolution, natural selection and adaptation; ecosystems; (Earth Science) climate change; (ELA) integration of knowledge and ideas (RST.6-8.7-.9)

Major Products: Research notebooks; written and illustrated pages for website; oral presentation

Public Audience: other science teachers; representative of state wildlife agency

---

Elementary Example:

Project Title: What am I?

Grade: Kindergarten

Project Idea: Students study what it means to be "alive" and learn by observation, listening and reading what makes animals different from plants. They reflect on what they themselves are, but also how they share some characteristics of plants too ("I like to turn toward the sun!" or "I need water") as they create a picture book.

DQ: Are animals like plants or are they different?

Content: (ELA) reading informational text: ask and answer key ideas and details (RI.K.1-3); informative writing (W.K.2/K.7); (Biological Science) what distinguishes living from non-living things; characteristics of animal and plant life

Major Products: picture book with text, showing the differences and similarities between animals and plants, with the children's reflections about themselves

Public Audience: parents and visitors to the school's "Science Wall" display

3. Problem-solving Situation

Secondary Example:

Project Title: Grub Up!

Grade: 11-12

Project Idea: Students act as consultants who need to help a small business transform an old restaurant in their community into one that is more up-to-date and profitable. (May use case studies or actual local restaurants.)

DQ: How can we update an old restaurant?

Content: (Career/Tech) budgeting, pricing, business plan, market analysis, advertising, food service; (ELA) informative writing (W.11-12.12a-f); research projects (W.11-12.7-.8); presentation of knowledge and ideas (SL.11-12.4-.6)

Major Products: Business plan; cover letter; oral presentation with visual aids; sample marketing & advertising materials; sample menus

Public Audience: owners of the business (role-played or real)

Elementary Example:

Project Title: Go Mice Go!

Grade: 1

Project Idea: Students find out that mice are living in the school building and decide what to do about the situation. They learn about how mice live in this habitat, make estimates of how many mice there might be, draw pictures and read & write stories about mice. They study different ways to deal with mice in a building and make a recommendation in a presentation.

DQ: What should we do about the mice in our school?

Content: (Math) adding and subtracting whole numbers (NBT.C.4); (Biological Science) habitat, basic requirements for life; (ELA) narrative writing (W.1.3); shared research (W.1.7)

Major Products: storybook about mice; presentation of recommendations

Public Audience: school principal & custodian, district representative

4. Examination of a Controversial Issue

Secondary Example:

Project Title: Get'em If They Smoke'em

Grade: 12

Project Idea: Students research the relevant political, economic, and social issues as they weigh the pros and cons of raising taxes on cigarettes. They draw conclusions and write persuasive essays in the form of op-ed pieces for local print and online media and letters to state legislators.

DQ: Should we raise taxes on cigarettes?

Content: (Government) state government, taxation, public health policy; (ELA) argumentative writing (W.11-12.1a-e); informative writing (W.11-12.2a-f)

Major Products: Research report; persuasive essays

Public Audience: Readers of print and online media; state legislators

Elementary Example:

Project Title: To Bus or Not To Bus

Grade: 5

Project Idea: Since the district is considering the elimination of school bus service, students study the issue and make recommendations. They interview administrators, survey parents, collect data, and write reports, which they summarize and present at a school board meeting.

DQ: Should our school keep the buses?

Content: (Math) fractions (NF.A-B), decimals (NBT.A.1); (ELA) opinion writing (W.5.1a-d); presentation of knowledge and ideas (SL.5.4-.6)

Major Products: Written report and presentation to district administrators & school board

Public Audience: district administrators & school board

5. Challenge to Design, Plan, Produce or Create Something

Secondary Example:

Project Title: Equations of Art

Grade: 8

Project Idea: The principal feels the school lacks visual artifacts of school spirit and culture, so she asks students for proposals for an interdisciplinary mural for the wall near her office. Student teams use algebra to design murals and principles of art to create prototypes.

DQ: How can we use algebra to artistically showcase our school spirit?

Content: (Math) linear equations, graphing, coordinate points, slope of a line (EE.B.5); (Art) mural design and materials, use of color and shape; (ELA) presentation of knowledge and ideas (SL.8.4-.6)

Major Products: linear equations for mural design; written design rationale; design pitch presentation

Public Audience: school leadership team and staff members

Elementary Example:

Project Title: Local Pride!

Grade: 3

Project Idea: Students learn about the history of their community through field trips, guest speakers, interviews with residents, and reading primary source documents. Working in teams, they write reports on various topics, create exhibits focused on different aspects of their history—economic, social, and geographic—which are displayed at an evening event they plan for the community.

DQ: How can we create museum exhibits and plan an event that explains and celebrates the history of our community?

Content: (Social Studies) local and state history; (ELA) reading informational text (RI.3.1-.6); informative writing (W.3.2a-d); (Math) geometric measure (G.A.2 & MD.D.8)

Major Products: research report; visual display, with written explanations of visual elements; community event

Public Audience: parents and community members attending the evening event

What to learn: 'core knowledge' or '21st-century skills'?

By Greg Toppo

March 5, 2009

WASHINGTON — If someone told you that kids need to think critically and creatively, be technologically savvy and work well with others, you'd nod in agreement, right?

At least 10 states (note: 45 as of 2012) have committed to helping students develop these "21st-century skills" in schools, the workplace and beyond… working with the Arizona-based Partnership for 21st Century Skills, or P21, the movement's main advocacy group.

But a small group of outspoken education scholars is challenging that assumption, saying the push for 21st-century skills is taking a dangerous bite out of precious classroom time that could be better spent learning deep, essential content. For the first time since the P21 push began seven years ago, they're pushing back. In a forum here last week they squared off with education consultant Ken Kay, co-founder of the P21 movement.

"It's an ineffectual use of school time," says E.D. Hirsch Jr., founder of the Core Knowledge Foundation and author of a series of books on what students should learn year-by-year in school. He calls the P21 movement "a fragmented approach with uncertain cognitive goals" that could most profoundly hurt disadvantaged children: At home, he says, they don't get as much background as middle-class students in history, science, literature and the like.

Core Knowledge holds that an explicit, grade-by-grade "core of common learning" is necessary for a good education. So, for instance, when fifth-graders learn about Galileo's role in astronomy, they study Italian history and geography as well.

Kay calls criticisms by Hirsch and others "a sideshow that distracts people from the issue at hand: that our kids need world-class skills and world-class content."

Kay notes that virtually all of the industrialized countries the USA is competing with "are pursuing both content and skills."

At its heart, say Hirsch and others, the conflict is about what should happen in a school day: Do kids learn to think by reading great literature, doing difficult math and learning history, philosophy and science? Or can they tackle those subjects on their own if schools simply teach them to problem-solve, communicate, use technology and think creatively?

If you pursue the latter, says University of Virginia cognitive psychologist Daniel Willingham, the rich content you're after inevitably "falls by the wayside." While kids may enjoy working together on projects, for instance, the amount of knowledge they get often ends up being shallow. Furthermore, he says, research shows that many teachers find it difficult to actually teach children to think creatively or collaborate. In the end, they rarely get better at the very skills that P21 advocates.

"If we want our kids to learn how to be better collaborators, we're going to need to teach that," says Willingham, author of the new book Why Don't Students Like School?.

Kay says P21 critics miss the point, offering "a false choice" that won't help U.S. students. He says he hopes to work with critics on incorporating both thinking skills and content into future P21 work. "We need kids who don't just do what they're told but who are self-directed," he says.

Bianca Hewes

D.I.Y. teaching and learning

Posted on **June 6, 2011**

Is my PBL faux student-centred learning?

Last Thursday afternoon I had the pleasure of running a video conference with a couple of other schools to talk about Edmodo. I was particularly excited about this video conference because I could finally meet Neil Fara face to face. Neil is a really inspiring teacher who is running a really innovative experiment he refers to as Project REAL. You can read a little about it at the Edmodo Teacher Hub. Anyway, long story short, Neil and I had been chatting via yammer for a few weeks leading up to the VC – Neil is interested in what I do with PBL and I'm interested in what he's doing in regards to student voice.

So the video conference ran really smoothly … Neil and the other participants let me blabber on for about half an hour about how my students are using Edmodo as the hub for their projects and just showing them around my crazy busy Edmodo page. I have to confess, I was feeling a little like a tech-savvy PBL guru.

And then it hit. BAM!

Neil asked me this: Do you let your students plan these projects? Do they look at the outcomes? Do they get a say in the products and investigations?

I pretty much stuttered and blundered my answer, something eloquent like 'Ah, nah. It's pretty much all me doing that stuff. Yeah. Hmmm…'

My debrief has been slow. I haven't really shared it with anyone. Here's the realisation: What I'm doing with 'PBL' isn't really student-centred. Is it? If I'm in control of designing the project – from crafting the question, designing the products and investigations and organising the 'real world' audience to present to – then it's totally teacher-centred. If I'm the one who allocates the points as rewards, then I'm the boss, right?

Despite the demon that sits on my shoulder and tells me I'm a fraud, there is a voice somewhere amongst the din that says 'It's a continuum. They have un-learned passive learning. They have learnt to plan and reflect. They are excelling at team work. They are more motivated than ever. You now know your students better than you ever have. Next stop is student voice. It takes time.'

I really want to listen to that voice. I do.

Posted June 6, 2011 By Bianca Hewes, a teacher in Australia, at **http://biancahewes.wordpress.com/**

Blog

May 24, 2012

What Does It Take for a Project to be "Authentic"?

John Larmer, BIE

Everyone thinks that Project Based Learning has something to do with "authentic" learning. But not everyone agrees what this means. I think there could be a sliding scale of authenticity in PBL.

"Not authentic" means the work students do does not resemble the kind of work done in the world outside of school or it is not intended to have an effect on anything apart from an academic purpose. A not-authentic project would involve the kind of assignment students are typically given in school: compose an essay, create a poster or model, write and present a book report, or make a PowerPoint presentation on a topic they've researched. Beyond their teacher and maybe their classmates there's no public audience for students' work, no one actually uses what they create, and the work they do is not what people do in the real world.

"Somewhat authentic" means students are doing work that simulates what happens in the world outside of school. In a project that is somewhat authentic, students could play a role: scientists, engineers, advisors to the President, or website designers who are placed in a scenario that reflects what might actually occur in the real world. Or students could create products that, although they are not actually going to be used by people in the real world, are the kinds of products people do use or create.

"Fully authentic" means students are doing work that is real to them — it is authentic to their lives — or the work has a direct impact on or use in the real world. The "real world," by the way, could still be school, which is a very real place for students. In these projects, students might advocate for a cause; take action to improve their community; perform a service for someone; create a physical artifact to display or distribute, or express their own ideas about a topic in various media for particular audiences.

A project can be authentic in four ways, some of which may be combined in one project:

1. **It meets a real need in the world beyond the classroom or the products students create are used by real people.**
   - ▶ Students propose designs for a new play area in a nearby park.
   - ▶ Students plan and execute an environmental clean-up effort in their community.
   - ▶ Students create a website for young people about books they like.
   - ▶ Students write a guide and produce podcasts for visitors to historic sites in their city.
   - ▶ Students serve as consultants to local businesses, advising them on how to increase sales to young people.
   - ▶ Students develop a conflict resolution plan for their school.

2. **It focuses on a problem, issue, or topic that is relevant to students' lives — the more directly, the better — or on a problem or issue that is actually being faced by adults in the world students will soon enter.**
   - ▶ Students create multimedia presentations that explore the question, "How do we make and lose friends?"
   - ▶ Students learn physics by investigating the question, "Why don't I fall off my skateboard?"
   - ▶ Students learn about stray pets in their community and recommend what people should do.
   - ▶ Students decide whether the U.S. should intervene in a conflict inside another country.

3. **It sets up a scenario or simulation that is realistic, even if it is fictitious.**
   - ▶ Students are asked by the Archbishop of Mexico in 1819 to recommend a location for the next mission in California.
   - ▶ Students act as architects designing a theatre that holds the maximum number of people, given certain constraints.
   - ▶ Students are United Nations advisors to a country that needs advice about how to start a democracy.
   - ▶ Students recommend which planet should be explored by the next space probe as they compete for NASA funding.
   - ▶ Students are asked to propose ideas for a new TV reality show that educates viewers about science topics.

4. **It involves tools, tasks, or processes used by adults in real settings and by professionals in the workplace. (This type of authenticity could apply to any of the above examples of projects.)**
   - ▶ Students investigating the physics of skateboarding test various surfaces for speed, using the scientific method and tools scientists use.
   - ▶ Students exploring the issue of how we make and lose friends conduct surveys, analyze data, record video interviews, and use online editing tools to assemble their presentations.
   - ▶ Students acting as U.N advisors to an emerging democracy analyze existing constitutions, write formal reports, and present recommendations to a panel.

I agree with purists that fully authentic projects are usually the most powerful and effective ones, because they are so engaging for students and allow them to feel like they can have an impact on their world — so the more of them, the better. But if you can't get there yet, don't feel like you're failing the authenticity test in your projects. Some is still better than none!

Driving Question TUBRIC 2.0™

Framing Words	Person or Entity	Action or Challenge	Audience or Purpose

TUBRIC™ | bie.org

Assembly required.
Instructions not included.
Application open-ended
It's Project Based Learning.

1	2	3	4
[Wild Card]	[Wild Card]	[Wild Card]	[Wild Card]
How can...	I / We	Build... Create... Make...	Real-World Problem
How do...	We as, [Roles] [Occupations]	Design... Plan...	For a Public Audience
Should...	[Town] [City] [County]	Solve...	For a School
Could...	[State] [Nation]	Write...	For a Classroom
What...	[Community] [Organization]	Propose... Decide...	For an Online Audience

TUBRIC™ | bie.org

PBL Essential Elements Checklist

Whatever form a project takes, it must have these Essential Elements to meet BIE's definition of PBL.

Does the Project . . .?	👍	👎	?
FOCUS ON SIGNIFICANT CONTENT At its core, the project is focused on teaching students important knowledge and skills, derived from standards and key concepts at the heart of academic subjects.			
DEVELOP 21st CENTURY COMPETENCIES Students build competencies valuable for today's world, such as critical thinking/problem solving, collaboration, and communication, and creativity/ innovation, which are taught and assessed.	✓		
ENGAGE STUDENTS IN IN-DEPTH INQUIRY Students are engaged in a rigorous, extended process of asking questions, using resources, and developing answers.	✓		
ORGANIZE TASKS AROUND A DRIVING QUESTION Project work is focused by an open-ended question that students understand and find intriguing, which captures their task or frames their exploration.			✓
ESTABLISH A NEED TO KNOW Students see the need to gain knowledge, understand concepts, and apply skills in order to answer the Driving Question and create project products, beginning with an Entry Event that generates interest and curiosity.		✓	
ENCOURAGE VOICE AND CHOICE Students are allowed to make some choices about the products to be created, how they work, and how they use their time, guided by the teacher and depending on age level and PBL experience.		✓	
INCORPORATE CRITIQUE AND REVISION The project includes processes for students to give and receive feedback on the quality of their work, leading them to make revisions or conduct further inquiry.	✓		
INCLUDE A PUBLIC AUDIENCE Students present their work to other people, beyond their classmates and teacher.	✓		

PBL Essential Elements Checklist

Whatever form a project takes, it must have these Essential Elements to meet BIE's definition of PBL.

Does the Project . . .?	👍	👎	?
FOCUS ON SIGNIFICANT CONTENT At its core, the project is focused on teaching students important knowledge and skills, derived from standards and key concepts at the heart of academic subjects.			
DEVELOP 21st CENTURY COMPETENCIES Students build competencies valuable for today's world, such as critical thinking/problem solving, collaboration, and communication, and creativity/ innovation, which are taught and assessed.			
ENGAGE STUDENTS IN IN-DEPTH INQUIRY Students are engaged in a rigorous, extended process of asking questions, using resources, and developing answers.			
ORGANIZE TASKS AROUND A DRIVING QUESTION Project work is focused by an open-ended question that students understand and find intriguing, which captures their task or frames their exploration.			
ESTABLISH A NEED TO KNOW Students see the need to gain knowledge, understand concepts, and apply skills in order to answer the Driving Question and create project products, beginning with an Entry Event that generates interest and curiosity.			
ENCOURAGE VOICE AND CHOICE Students are allowed to make some choices about the products to be created, how they work, and how they use their time, guided by the teacher and depending on age level and PBL experience.			
INCORPORATE CRITIQUE AND REVISION The project includes processes for students to give and receive feedback on the quality of their work, leading them to make revisions or conduct further inquiry.			
INCLUDE A PUBLIC AUDIENCE Students present their work to other people, beyond their classmates and teacher.			

No School Tomorrow!

Cut out and arrange the disaster warning signs in order from "least likely" to "most likely" to happen. Your team must agree on the order.

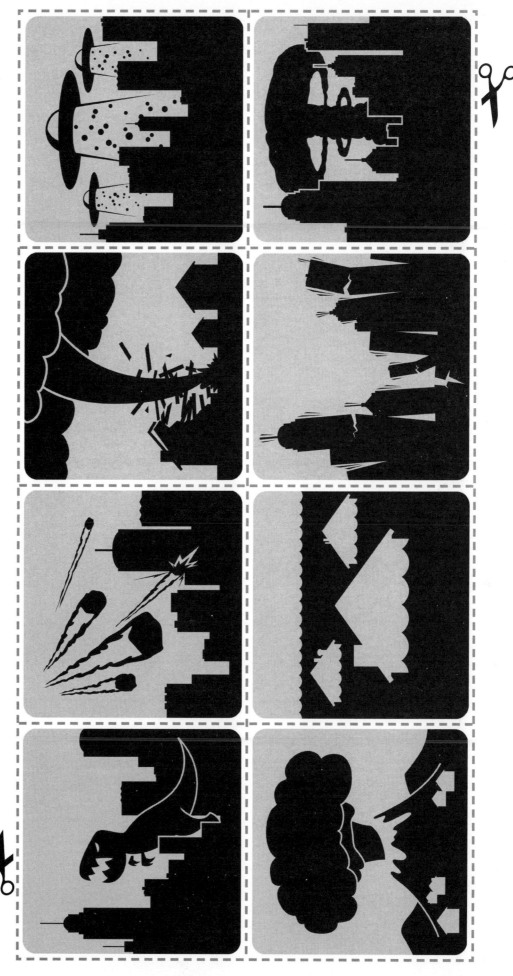

PROJECT DESIGN RUBRIC

| Essential Element of PBL | Lacks Essential Features of Effective PBL
The project has one or more of the following problems in each area: | Needs Further Development
The project has essential PBL features but has some of the following weaknesses: | Incorporates Best PBL Practices
The project has the following strengths: |
|---|---|---|---|
| **Significant Content** | ▶ The project is not aligned with standards and what students learn is not important in terms of concepts from academic subject areas. | ▶ The project is aligned with standards and concepts from academic subject areas, but it may focus on too few, too many, or less important ones. | ▶ The project is focused on teaching students important knowledge and skills derived from standards and key concepts at the heart of academic subject areas. |
| **21st Century Competencies** | ▶ The development of 21st century competencies is not included.
▶ It is assumed that some 21st century competencies will be gained by students, but the project does not explicitly scaffold the development of these competencies.
▶ Students do all project tasks as individuals.
▶ Students are not asked to think critically or solve problems.
▶ Students are not given opportunities to use creativity or follow a process for innovation.
Note: For Communication see ***Public Audience.*** | ▶ Too few or relatively unimportant competencies are targeted, OR too many to be adequately taught & assessed.
▶ The project scaffolds the development of 21st century competencies to some extent, but there may not be adequate opportunities to build competencies or rigorously assess them.
▶ Students work in teams, but it may be more cooperative than collaborative (the work of individuals is pieced together).
▶ Students are asked to analyze & solve problems and think critically, but not in depth or in a sustained way.
▶ Students may find ways to be creative and innovative, but without using a process. | ▶ A limited number of important 21st century competencies are targeted to be taught & assessed.
▶ There are adequate opportunities to build 21st century competencies and they are rigorously assessed (with a rubric and feedback).
▶ Students work in collaborative teams that employ the skills of all group members; students may collaborate with people beyond their classmates.
▶ Students are asked to analyze & solve problems and think critically, in an in-depth and sustained way.
▶ Students are given opportunities to use creativity and follow a process for innovation. |
| **In-Depth Inquiry** | ▶ The "project" is more like an activity or applied learning task, rather than an extended inquiry.
▶ The "project" is unfocused, more like a unit with several tasks than one project. | ▶ Inquiry is superficial (information-gathering is the main task).
▶ Inquiry focuses on only one too-narrow topic, OR it tries to include too many issues, side topics, or tasks. | ▶ Inquiry is sustained and academically rigorous: students pose questions, gather & interpret data, ask further questions, and develop & evaluate solutions or build evidence for answers. |
| **Driving Question** | ▶ There is no DQ.
▶ DQ is seriously flawed; for example:
  - It has a single or simple answer.
  - It is not engaging to students (it sounds too "academic," like it came from a textbook or appeals only to a teacher). | ▶ DQ relates to the project but does not capture its main focus; it may be more like a theme.
▶ DQ meets some criteria for an effective DQ, but lacks others (it may lead students toward one particular answer, or it may be hard to answer thoroughly with the resources & time available and/or by students in this class). | ▶ DQ captures the project 's main focus.
▶ DQ is open-ended; it allows for students to develop more than one reasonable, complex answer.
▶ DQ is understandable & inspiring to students.
▶ To answer the DQ, students will need to gain the intended knowledge, skills, & understanding. |

Need to Know	▼ The project does not motivate students to learn new content knowledge or gain skills. ▼ No Entry Event is planned. Day one of the project will feel like any other day (or worse, because it seems like more work than usual).	▼ The project motivates students to learn new content knowledge or gain skills because they see the need for them in order to complete project products and not be embarrassed to present their work. ▼ The Entry Event will gain student attention but it will not begin the inquiry process by creating a "need to know" or generate questions about the topic of the project.	▼ The project motivates students to learn new content knowledge or gain skills because they genuinely find the project's topic, Driving Question, and tasks to be relevant and meaningful. ▼ The Entry Event will powerfully engage students, both emotionally & intellectually (make them feel invested in the project & provoke inquiry)
Voice & Choice	▼ Students are not given opportunities, if appropriate, to express "voice & choice" (to make decisions affecting the content or conduct of the project). ▼ Students are expected to work too much on their own, without adequate guidance from the teacher and/or before they are capable.	▼ Students are given limited opportunities to express "voice & choice," generally with less important matters (deciding how to divide tasks within a team or which website to use for research). ▼ Students are expected to work independently from the teacher to some extent, although they have the skills and desire to do even more on their own.	▼ Students have opportunities to express "voice & choice" on important matters (the topics to study, questions asked, texts & resources used, products created, use of time, and organization of tasks). ▼ Students have opportunities to take significant responsibility and work independently from the teacher.
Critique & Revision	▼ Students do not give and receive feedback about their work-in-progress. ▼ Students are not taught how to give constructive critique of each other's work-in-progress (it is brief, superficial, vague). ▼ Students do not use feedback about the quality of their work to revise and improve it.	▼ Students are provided with opportunities to give and receive feedback about the quality of their work-in-progress, but they may be unstructured or only occur once. ▼ Students are given brief, general guidelines for critiquing each other's work-in-progress. ▼ Students look at and/or listen to feedback about the quality of their work, but do not substantially revise and improve it.	▼ Students are provided with regular, structured opportunities to give and receive feedback about the quality of their work-in-progress. ▼ Students are taught how to constructively critique each other's work-in-progress. ▼ Students use feedback about the quality of their work to revise and improve it.
Public Audience	▼ Students do not share, present or exhibit their work.	▼ Students share their work only with classmates & the teacher. ▼ Students present culminating products, but their explanation of how & why they did things is limited to a short, superficial question/answer session.	▼ Students share their work with other people from both within and outside the school, which may include online audiences. ▼ Students present culminating products and defend them in detail & in depth (by explaining their reasoning behind choices they made, their inquiry process, etc.).

COLLABORATION RUBRIC for PBL
(for grades 6-12; CCSS ELA aligned)

Individual Performance	Below Standard	Approaching Standard	At Standard	Above Standard ✔
Takes Responsibility for Oneself	▶ is not prepared, informed, and ready to work with the team ▶ does not use technology tools as agreed upon by the team to communicate and manage project tasks ▶ does not do project tasks ▶ does not complete tasks on time ▶ does not use feedback from others to improve work	▶ is usually prepared, informed, and ready to work with the team ▶ uses technology tools as agreed upon by the team to communicate and manage project tasks, but not consistently ▶ does some project tasks, but needs to be reminded ▶ completes most tasks on time ▶ sometimes uses feedback from others to improve work	▶ is prepared and ready to work; is well informed on the project topic and cites evidence to probe and reflect on ideas with the team (CC 6-12.SL.1a) ▶ consistently uses technology tools as agreed upon by the team to communicate and manage project tasks ▶ does tasks without having to be reminded ▶ completes tasks on time ▶ uses feedback from others to improve work	
Helps the Team	▶ does not help the team solve problems; may cause problems ▶ does not ask probing questions, express ideas, or elaborate in response to questions in discussions ▶ does not give useful feedback to others ▶ does not offer to help others if they need it	▶ cooperates with the team but may not actively help it solve problems ▶ sometimes expresses ideas clearly, asks probing questions, and elaborates in response to questions in discussions ▶ gives feedback to others, but it may not always be useful ▶ sometimes offers to help others if they need it	▶ helps the team solve problems and manage conflicts ▶ makes discussions effective by clearly expressing ideas, asking probing questions, making sure everyone is heard, responding thoughtfully to new information and perspectives (CC 6-12.SL.1c) ▶ gives useful feedback (specific, feasible, supportive) to others so they can improve their work ▶ offers to help others do their work if needed	
Respects Others	▶ is impolite or unkind to teammates (may interrupt, ignore ideas, hurt feelings) ▶ does not acknowledge or respect other perspectives	▶ is usually polite and kind to teammates ▶ usually acknowledges and respects other perspectives and disagrees diplomatically	▶ is polite and kind to teammates ▶ acknowledges and respects other perspectives; disagrees diplomatically	

Team Performance	Below Standard	Approaching Standard	At Standard	Above Standard ✔
Makes and Follows Agreements	▸ does not discuss how the team will work together ▸ does not follow rules for collegial discussions, decision-making and conflict resolution ▸ does not discuss how well agreements are being followed ▸ allows breakdowns in team work to happen; needs teacher to intervene	▸ discusses how the team will work together, but not in detail; may just "go through the motions" when creating an agreement ▸ usually follows rules for collegial discussions, decision-making, and conflict resolution ▸ discusses how well agreements are being followed, but not in depth; may ignore subtle issues ▸ notices when norms are not being followed but asks the teacher for help to resolve issues	▸ makes detailed agreements about how the team will work together, including the use of technology tools ▸ follows rules for collegial discussions (CC 6-12.SL.1b), decision-making, and conflict resolution ▸ honestly and accurately discusses how well agreements are being followed ▸ takes appropriate action when norms are not being followed; attempts to resolve issues without asking the teacher for help	
Organizes Work	▸ does project work without creating a task list ▸ does not set a schedule and track progress toward goals and deadlines ▸ does not assign roles or share leadership; one person may do too much, or all members may do random tasks ▸ wastes time and does not run meetings well; materials, drafts, notes are not organized (may be misplaced or inaccessible)	▸ creates a task list that divides project work among the team, but it may not be in detail or followed closely ▸ sets a schedule for doing tasks but does not follow it closely ▸ assigns roles but does not follow them, or selects only one "leader" who makes most decisions ▸ usually uses time and runs meetings well, but may occasionally waste time; keeps materials, drafts, notes, but not always organized	▸ creates a detailed task list that divides project work reasonably among the team ▸ sets a schedule and tracks progress toward goals and deadlines (CC 6-12.SL.1b) ▸ assigns roles if and as needed, based on team members' strengths (CC 6-12.SL.1b) ▸ uses time and runs meetings efficiently; keeps materials, drafts, notes organized	
Works as a Whole Team	▸ does not recognize or use special talents of team members ▸ does project tasks separately and does not put them together; it is a collection of individual work	▸ makes some attempt to use special talents of team members ▸ does most project tasks separately and puts them together at the end	▸ recognizes and uses special talents of each team member ▸ develops ideas and creates products with involvement of all team members; tasks done separately are brought to the team for critique and revision	

CREATIVITY & INNOVATION RUBRIC for PBL

(for grades 6-12; CCSS ELA aligned)

PROCESS

Creativity & Innovation Opportunity at Phases of a Project	Below Standard	Approaching Standard	At Standard	Above Standard ✔
Launching the Project **Define the Creative Challenge**	▸ may just "follow directions" without understanding the purpose for innovation or considering the needs and interests of the target audience	▸ understands the basic purpose for innovation but does not thoroughly consider the needs and interests of the target audience	▸ understands the purpose driving the process of innovation (Who needs this? Why?) ▸ develops insight about the particular needs and interests of the target audience	
Building Knowledge, Understanding, and Skills **Identify Sources of Information**	▸ uses only typical sources of information (website, book, article) ▸ does not offer new ideas during discussions	▸ finds one or two sources of information that are not typical ▸ offers new ideas during discussions, but stays within narrow perspectives	▸ in addition to typical sources, finds unusual ways or places to get information (adult expert, community member, business or organization, literature) ▸ promotes divergent and creative perspectives during discussions (CC 11-12.SL.1c)	
Developing and Revising Ideas and Products **Generate and Select Ideas**	▸ stays within existing frameworks; does not use idea-generating techniques to develop new ideas for product(s) ▸ selects one idea without evaluating the quality of ideas ▸ does not ask new questions or elaborate on the selected idea ▸ reproduces existing ideas; does not imagine new ones ▸ does not consider or use feedback and critique to revise product	▸ develops some original ideas for product(s), but could develop more with better use of idea-generating techniques ▸ evaluates ideas, but not thoroughly before selecting one ▸ asks a few new questions but may make only minor changes to the selected idea ▸ shows some imagination when shaping ideas into a product, but may stay within conventional boundaries ▸ considers and may use some feedback and critique to revise a product, but does not seek it out	▸ uses idea-generating techniques to develop several original ideas for product(s) ▸ carefully evaluates the quality of ideas and selects the best one to shape into a product ▸ asks new questions, takes different perspectives to elaborate and improve on the selected idea ▸ uses ingenuity and imagination, going outside conventional boundaries, when shaping ideas into a product ▸ seeks out and uses feedback and critique to revise product to better meet the needs of the intended audience (CC 6-12.W.5)	
Presenting Products and Answers to Driving Question **Present Work to Users/Target Audience**	▸ presents ideas and products in typical ways (text-heavy PowerPoint slides, recitation of notes, no interactive features)	▸ adds some interesting touches to presentation media ▸ attempts to include elements in presentation that make it more lively and engaging	▸ creates visually exciting presentation media ▸ includes elements in presentation that are especially fun, lively, engaging, or powerful to the particular audience	

PRODUCT

	Below Standard	Approaching Standard	At Standard	Above Standard ✔
Originality	▸ relies on existing models, ideas, or directions; it is not new or unique ▸ follows rules and conventions; uses materials and ideas in typical ways	▸ has some new ideas or improvements, but some ideas are predictable or conventional ▸ may show a tentative attempt to step outside rules and conventions, or find new uses for common materials or ideas	▸ is new, unique, surprising; shows a personal touch ▸ may successfully break rules and conventions, or use common materials or ideas in new, clever and surprising ways	
Value	▸ is not useful or valuable to the intended audience/user ▸ would not work in the real world; impractical or unfeasible	▸ is useful and valuable to some extent; it may not solve certain aspects of the defined problem or exactly meet the identified need ▸ unclear if product would be practical or feasible	▸ is seen as useful and valuable; it solves the defined problem or meets the identified need ▸ is practical, feasible	
Style	▸ is safe, ordinary, made in a conventional style ▸ has several elements that do not fit together; it is a mish-mash	▸ has some interesting touches, but lacks a distinct style ▸ has some elements that may be excessive or do not fit together well	▸ is well-crafted, striking, designed with a distinct style but still appropriate for the purpose ▸ combines different elements into a coherent whole	

Note: The term "product" is used in this rubric as an umbrella term for the result of the process of innovation during a project. A product may be a constructed object, proposal, presentation, solution to a problem, service, system, work of art or piece of writing, an invention, event, an improvement to an existing product, etc.

CRITICAL THINKING RUBRIC for PBL

(for grades 6-12; CCSS ELA aligned)

Critical Thinking Opportunity at Phases of a Project	Below Standard	Approaching Standard	At Standard	Above Standard ✓
Launching the Project: **Analyze Driving Question and Begin Inquiry**	▸ sees only superficial aspects of, or one point of view on, the Driving Question	▸ identifies some central aspects of the Driving Question, but may not see complexities or consider various points of view ▸ asks some follow-up questions about the topic or the wants and needs of the audience or users of a product, but does not dig deep	▸ shows understanding of central aspects of the Driving Question by identifying in detail what needs to be known to answer it and considering various possible points of view on it ▸ asks follow-up questions that focus or broaden inquiry, as appropriate (CC 6-12.W.7) ▸ asks follow-up questions to gain understanding of the wants and needs of audience or product users	
Building Knowledge, Understanding, and Skills: **Gather and Evaluate Information**	▸ is unable to integrate information to address the Driving Question; gathers too little, too much, or irrelevant information, or from too few sources ▸ accepts information at face value (does not evaluate its quality)	▸ attempts to integrate information to address the Driving Question, but it may be too little, too much, or gathered from too few sources; some of it may not be relevant ▸ understands that the quality of information should be considered, but does not do so thoroughly	▸ integrates relevant and sufficient information to address the Driving Question, gathered from multiple and varied sources (CC 6,11-12.RI.7) ▸ thoroughly assesses the quality of information (considers usefulness, accuracy and credibility; distinguishes fact vs. opinion; recognizes bias) (CC 6-12.W.8)	
Developing and Revising Ideas and Products: **Use Evidence and Criteria**	▸ accepts arguments for possible answers to the Driving Question without questioning whether reasoning is valid ▸ uses evidence without considering how strong it is ▸ relies on "gut feeling" to evaluate and revise ideas, product prototypes or problem solutions (does not use criteria)	▸ recognizes the need for valid reasoning and strong evidence, but does not evaluate it carefully when developing answers to the Driving Question ▸ evaluates and revises ideas, product prototypes or problem solutions based on incomplete or invalid criteria	▸ evaluates arguments for possible answers to the Driving Question by assessing whether reasoning is valid and evidence is relevant and sufficient (CC 6-12.SL.3, RI.8) ▸ justifies choice of criteria used to evaluate ideas, product prototypes or problem solutions ▸ revises inadequate drafts, designs or solutions and explains why they will better meet evaluation criteria (CC 6-12.W.5)	
Presenting Products and Answers to Driving Question: **Justify Choices, Consider Alternatives & Implications**	▸ chooses one presentation medium without considering advantages and disadvantages of using other mediums to present a particular topic or idea ▸ cannot give valid reasons or supporting evidence to defend choices made when answering the Driving Question or creating products ▸ does not consider alternative answers to the Driving Question, designs for products, or points of view ▸ is not able to explain important new understanding gained in the project	▸ considers the advantages and disadvantages of using different mediums to present a particular topic or idea, but not thoroughly ▸ explains choices made when answering the Driving Question or creating products, but some reasons are not valid or lack supporting evidence ▸ understands that there may be alternative answers to the Driving Question or designs for products, but does not consider them carefully ▸ can explain some things learned in the project, but is not entirely clear about new understanding	▸ evaluates the advantages and disadvantages of using different mediums to present a particular topic or idea (CC 8.RI.7) ▸ justifies choices made when answering the Driving Question or creating products, by giving valid reasons with supporting evidence (CC 6-12.SL.4) ▸ recognizes the limitations of an answer to the Driving Question or a product design (how it might not be complete, certain, or perfect) and considers alternative perspectives (CC 11-12.SL.4) ▸ can clearly explain new understanding gained in the project and how it might transfer to other situations or contexts	

Presentation Rubric
(for grades K-2)

I plan a beginning, middle, and end.

1. still learning

2. sometimes

3. almost always

I use pictures, drawings, and props.

1. still learning

2. sometimes

3. almost always

I look at my audience.

1. still learning

2. sometimes

3. almost always

I speak loudly and clearly.

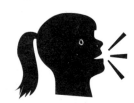

1. still learning

2. sometimes

3. almost always

I answer questions from the audience.

1. still learning

2. sometimes

3. almost always

PRESENTATION RUBRIC for PBL

(for grades 3-5; Common Core ELA aligned)

	Below Standard	Approaching Standard	At Standard	Above Standard ✓
Explanation of Ideas & Information	▸ uses inappropriate facts and irrelevant details to support main ideas	▸ chooses some facts and details that support main ideas, but there may not be enough, or some are irrelevant	▸ chooses appropriate facts and relevant, descriptive details to support main ideas and themes (CC 3-5.SL.4)	
Organization	▸ does not include everything required in presentation ▸ presents ideas in an order that does not make sense ▸ does not plan timing of presentation well; it is too short or too long	▸ includes almost everything required in presentation ▸ tries to present ideas in an order, but it doesn't always makes sense ▸ presents for the right length of time, but some parts may be too short or too long	▸ includes everything required in presentation ▸ presents ideas in an order that makes sense (CC 3-5.SL.4) ▸ organizes time well; no part of the presentation is rushed, too short or too long	
Eyes & Body	▸ does not look at audience; reads notes ▸ fidgets or slouches a lot	▸ makes some eye contact, but reads notes or slides most of the time ▸ fidgets or slouches a little	▸ keeps eye contact with audience most of the time; only glances at notes or slides ▸ has a confident posture	
Voice	▸ speaks too quietly or not clearly ▸ does not speak appropriately for the situation (may be too informal or use slang)	▸ speaks loudly and clearly most of the time ▸ speaks appropriately for the situation most of the time	▸ speaks loudly and clearly ▸ speaks appropriately for the situation, using formal English when appropriate (CC 3-5.SL.6)	
Presentation Aids	▸ does not use audio/visual aids or media ▸ uses inappropriate or distracting audio/visual aids or media	▸ uses audio/visual aids or media, but they sometimes distract from the presentation, or do not add to ideas and themes	▸ uses well-produced audio/visual aids or media to add to main ideas and themes (CC 3-5.SL.5)	
Response to Audience Questions	▸ does not answer audience questions	▸ answers some audience questions, but not clearly or completely	▸ answers audience questions clearly and completely	
Participation in Team Presentations	▸ Not all team members participate; only one or two speak	▸ All team members participate, but not equally	▸ All team members participate for about the same length of time, and are able to answer questions	

PRESENTATION RUBRIC for PBL

(for grades 6-8; Common Core ELA aligned)

	Below Standard	Approaching Standard	At Standard	Above Standard ✔
Explanation of Ideas & Information	▸ uses too few, inappropriate, or irrelevant descriptions, facts, details, or examples to support ideas	▸ uses some descriptions, facts, details, and examples that support ideas, but there may not be enough, or some are irrelevant	▸ uses relevant, well-chosen descriptions, facts, details, and examples to support claims, findings, arguments, or an answer to a Driving Question (CC 6-8.SL.4)	
Organization	▸ does not include important parts required in the presentation ▸ does not have a main idea or presents ideas in an order that does not make sense ▸ does not have an introduction and/or conclusion ▸ uses time poorly; the whole presentation, or a part of it, is too short or too long	▸ includes almost everything required in the presentation ▸ moves from one idea to the next, but main idea may not be clear or some ideas may be in the wrong order ▸ has an introduction and conclusion, but they are not effective ▸ generally times presentation well, but may spend too much or too little time on a topic, a/v aid, or idea	▸ includes everything required in the presentation ▸ states main idea and moves from one idea to the next in a logical order, emphasizing main points in a focused, coherent manner (CC 6-8.SL.4) ▸ has an effective introduction and conclusion ▸ organizes time well; no part of the presentation is rushed, too short or too long	
Eyes & Body	▸ does not look at audience; reads notes or slides ▸ does not use gestures or movements ▸ lacks poise and confidence (fidgets, slouches, appears nervous) ▸ wears clothing inappropriate for the occasion	▸ makes infrequent eye contact; reads notes or slides most of the time ▸ uses a few gestures or movements but they do not look natural ▸ shows some poise and confidence (only a little fidgeting or nervous movement) ▸ makes some attempt to wear clothing appropriate for the occasion	▸ keeps eye contact with audience most of the time; only glances at notes or slides (CC 6-8.SL.4) ▸ uses natural gestures and movements ▸ looks poised and confident ▸ wears clothing appropriate for the occasion	
Voice	▸ mumbles or speaks too quickly or slowly ▸ speaks too softly to be understood ▸ frequently uses "filler" words ("uh, um, so, and, like, etc.") ▸ does not speak appropriately for the context and task (may be too informal, use slang)	▸ speaks clearly most of the time; sometimes too quickly or slowly ▸ speaks loudly enough for most of the audience to hear, but may speak in a monotone ▸ occasionally uses filler words ▸ tries to speak appropriately for the context and task	▸ speaks clearly; not too quickly or slowly (CC 6-8.SL.4) ▸ speaks loudly enough for everyone to hear; changes tone to maintain interest (CC 6-8.SL.4) ▸ rarely uses filler words ▸ speaks appropriately for the context and task, demonstrating command of formal English when appropriate (CC 6-8.SL.6)	

	Below Standard	Approaching Standard	At Standard	Above Standard ✔
Presentation Aids	▶ does not use audio/visual aids or media ▶ attempts to use one or a few audio/visual aids or media but they distract from or do not add to the presentation	▶ uses audio/visual aids or media, but they sometimes distract from or do not add to the presentation	▶ uses well-produced audio/visual aids or media to clarify information, emphasize important points, strengthen arguments, and add interest (CC 6-8.SL.5)	
Response to Audience Questions	▶ does not address audience questions (goes off topic or misunderstands without seeking clarification)	▶ answers some audience questions, but not always clearly or completely	▶ answers audience questions clearly and completely ▶ seeks clarification, admits "I don't know," or explains how the answer might be found when unable to answer a question	
Participation in Team Presentations	▶ Not all team members participate; only one or two speak	▶ All team members participate, but not equally	▶ All team members participate for about the same length of time ▶ All team members are able to answer questions about the topic as a whole, not just their part of it	

PRESENTATION RUBRIC for PBL
(for grades 9-12; Common Core ELA aligned)

	Below Standard	Approaching Standard	At Standard	Above Standard
Explanation of Ideas & Information	▼ does not present information, arguments, ideas, or findings clearly, concisely, and logically; argument lacks supporting evidence; audience cannot follow the line of reasoning ▼ selects information, develops ideas and uses a style inappropriate to the purpose, task, and audience (may be too much or too little information, or the wrong approach) ▼ does not address alternative or opposing perspectives	▼ presents information, findings, arguments and supporting evidence in a way that is not always clear, concise, and logical; line of reasoning is sometimes hard to follow ▼ attempts to select information, develop ideas and use a style appropriate to the purpose, task, and audience but does not fully succeed ▼ attempts to address alternative or opposing perspectives, but not clearly or completely	▼ presents information, findings, arguments and supporting evidence clearly, concisely, and logically; audience can easily follow the line of reasoning (CC 9-12.SL.4) ▼ selects information, develops ideas and uses a style appropriate to the purpose, task, and audience (CC 9-12.SL.4) ▼ clearly and completely addresses alternative or opposing perspectives (CC 11-12.SL.4)	✓
Organization	▼ does not meet requirements for what should be included in the presentation ▼ does not have an introduction and/or conclusion ▼ uses time poorly; the whole presentation, or a part of it, is too short or too long	▼ meets most requirements for what should be included in the presentation ▼ has an introduction and conclusion, but they are not clear or interesting ▼ generally times presentation well, but may spend too much or too little time on a topic, a/v aid, or idea	▼ meets all requirements for what should be included in the presentation ▼ has a clear and interesting introduction and conclusion ▼ organizes time well; no part of the presentation is too short or too long	9+i
Eyes & Body	▼ does not look at audience; reads notes or slides ▼ does not use gestures or movements ▼ lacks poise and confidence (fidgets, slouches, appears nervous) ▼ wears clothing inappropriate for the occasion	▼ makes infrequent eye contact; reads notes or slides most of the time ▼ uses a few gestures or movements but they do not look natural ▼ shows some poise and confidence, (only a little fidgeting or nervous movement) ▼ makes some attempt to wear clothing appropriate for the occasion	▼ keeps eye contact with audience most of the time; only glances at notes or slides ▼ uses natural gestures and movements ▼ looks poised and confident ▼ wears clothing appropriate for the occasion	9+.
Voice	▼ mumbles or speaks too quickly or slowly ▼ speaks too softly to be understood ▼ frequently uses "filler" words ("uh, um, so, and, like, etc.") ▼ does not adapt speech for the context and task	▼ speaks clearly most of the time ▼ speaks loudly enough for the audience to hear most of the time, but may speak in a monotone ▼ occasionally uses filler words ▼ attempts to adapt speech for the context and task but is unsuccessful or inconsistent	▼ speaks clearly; not too quickly or slowly ▼ speaks loudly enough for everyone to hear; changes tone and pace to maintain interest ▼ rarely uses filler words ▼ adapts speech for the context and task, demonstrating command of formal English when appropriate (CC 9-12.SL.6)	

	Below Standard	Approaching Standard	At Standard	Above Standard ✓
Presentation Aids	▶ does not use audio/visual aids or media ▶ attempts to use one or a few audio/visual aids or media, but they do not add to or may distract from the presentation	▶ uses audio/visual aids or media, but they may sometimes distract from or not add to the presentation ▶ sometimes has trouble bringing audio/visual aids or media smoothly into the presentation	▶ uses well-produced audio/visual aids or media to enhance understanding of findings, reasoning, and evidence, and to add interest (CC 9-12.SL.5) ▶ smoothly brings audio/visual aids or media into the presentation	
Response to Audience Questions	▶ does not address audience questions (goes off topic or misunderstands without seeking clarification)	▶ answers audience questions, but not always clearly or completely	▶ answers audience questions clearly and completely ▶ seeks clarification, admits "I don't know" or explains how the answer might be found when unable to answer a question	
Participation in Team Presentations	▶ Not all team members participate; only one or two speak	▶ All team members participate, but not equally	▶ All team members participate for about the same length of time ▶ All team members are able to answer questions about the topic as a whole, not just their part of it	

PROJECT DESIGN: OVERVIEW

page 1

Name of Project:	**Duration:**
Subject/Course:	**Teacher(s):**	**Grade Level:**

Other subject areas to be included, if any:

Significant Content (CCSS and/or others)	

21st Century Competencies (to be taught and assessed)	Collaboration	Creativity and Innovation
	Communication	Other:
	Critical Thinking	

Project Summary
(include student role,
issue, problem or
challenge, action taken,
and purpose/beneficiary)

Driving Question

Entry Event

Products	Individual:	Specific content and competencies to be assessed:
	Team:	Specific content and competencies to be assessed:

Public Audience
(Experts, audiences, or product users students will engage with during/at end of project)

Resources Needed		
On-site people, facilities:		
Equipment:		
Materials:		
Community Resources:		

Reflection Methods (Individual, Team, and/or Whole Class)			
Journal/Learning Log		Focus Group	
Whole-Class Discussion		Fishbowl Discussion	
Survey		Other:	

Notes:

PROJECT DESIGN: OVERVIEW

Name of Project:		Duration:
Subject/Course:	Teacher(s):	Grade Level:
Other subject areas to be included, if any:		

| Significant Content
(CCSS and/or others)		

| 21st Century
Competencies
(to be taught and
assessed)	Collaboration		Creativity and Innovation	
	Communication		Other:	
	Critical Thinking			

| Project Summary
(include student role,
issue, problem or
challenge, action taken,
and purpose/beneficiary)	

Driving Question	

Entry Event	

Products	Individual:	Specific content and competencies to be assessed:
	Team:	Specific content and competencies to be assessed:

Public Audience
(Experts, audiences, or product users students will engage with during/at end of project)

Resources Needed

On-site people, facilities:

Equipment:

Materials:

Community Resources:

Reflection Methods
(Individual, Team, and/or Whole Class)

Journal/Learning Log	Focus Group
Whole-Class Discussion	Fishbowl Discussion
Survey	Other:

Notes:

PROJECT DESIGN: STUDENT LEARNING GUIDE

Project:

Driving Question:

Final Product(s) Presentations, Performances, Products and/or Services	Learning Outcomes/Targets content & 21st century competencies needed by students to successfully complete products	Checkpoints/Formative Assessments to check for learning and ensure students are on track	Instructional Strategies for All Learners provided by teacher, other staff, experts; includes scaffolds, materials, lessons aligned to learning outcomes and formative assessments
(individual **and** team)			

PROJECT DESIGN: STUDENT LEARNING GUIDE

Project:

Driving Question:

Final Product(s) Presentations, Performances, Products and/or Services (individual **and** team)	Learning Outcomes/Targets content & 21st century competencies needed by students to successfully complete products	Checkpoints/Formative Assessments to check for learning and ensure students are on track	Instructional Strategies for All Learners provided by teacher, other staff, experts; includes scaffolds, materials, lessons aligned to learning outcomes and formative assessments

PROJECT CALENDAR

Project:

Time Frame:

MONDAY	TUESDAY	WEDNESDAY	THURSDAY	FRIDAY
		PROJECT WEEK ONE		

Notes

MONDAY	TUESDAY	WEDNESDAY	THURSDAY	FRIDAY
		PROJECT WEEK TWO		

Notes

Project:

Notes

MONDAY

TUESDAY

PROJECT WEEK THREE

WEDNESDAY

THURSDAY

FRIDAY

Notes

PROJECT WEEK FOUR

Project Journal

Name:

Date:

Rubric for Reflection

Skilled	Reflection is:
	▪ Thoughtful: Shows evidence of having deeply considered the issues, challenges, and successes in the project
	▪ Thorough: Reflects on multiple aspects of the project
	▪ Clear: Consistently expresses his or her thoughts in a way that is understandable to a reader

Reflection 1

Assessment in PBL is like a jigsaw puzzle. When each piece of assessment is completed and turned w/ the other pieces, it portrays a picture of what a student has learned and can do.

... also - like a map - to give the students direction.

Reflection 6

Reflection 7

Reflection 2

Reflection 3

Reflection 4

Reflection 5

PBL 101 Workshop Feedback

Name_____ Email _____

School _____ District _____

Your role
☐ Teacher
☐ Administrator
☐ Other:

_____

_____

Grade level
☐ Elementary
☐ Middle School
☐ High School
☐ Other:

_____

Subjects You Teach
☐ English
☐ Social Studies
☐ Science
☐ Math
☐ Other:

_____

The workshop was effective in helping me learn about PBL.
☐ Strongly agree
☐ Tend to agree
☐ Tend to disagree
☐ Strongly disagree

How do you feel about using PBL in your classroom?
☐ Very positive, encouraged
☐ Mostly positive, minor concerns
☐ Somewhat positive, but major concerns
☐ Very concerned, doubtful it will work for me

The facilitator was engaging.
☐ Strongly agree
☐ Tend to agree
☐ Tend to disagree
☐ Strongly disagree

The facilitator was knowledgeable about PBL.
☐ Strongly agree
☐ Tend to agree
☐ Tend to disagree
☐ Strongly disagree

The facilitator was helpful and responsive to participant needs and questions.
☐ Strongly agree
☐ Tend to agree
☐ Tend to disagree
☐ Strongly disagree

continued

BIE
BUCK INSTITUTE
FOR EDUCATION

The facilitator managed time and tasks well.

☐ Strongly agree
☐ Tend to agree
☐ Tend to disagree
☐ Strongly disagree

Additional feedback on facilitator.

```



```

Was there more than one facilitator for this workshop?

☐ Yes
☐ No

I still have questions or need help with:

☐ Driving Question
☐ Aligning project with standards
☐ Teaching and assessing 21st century competencies
☐ Formative assessment (checkpoints, feedback, critique, revision)
☐ Summative assessment (end of project, rubrics, peer and self assessment)
☐ Planning scaffolding and lessons
☐ Day to day planning on the calendar
☐ Managing teams
☐ Other:_____

Additional feedback on the workshop

```



```

☐ OPT OUT if you do NOT want to get email about new resources or opportunities.
☐ OPT OUT: If you do NOT wish to be quoted in our marketing materials.

BIE
BUCK INSTITUTE
FOR EDUCATION

Certificate of Completion

of

PBL 101

A 21-hour workshop in the design, assessment, and management of Project Based Learning by the Buck Institute for Education has been successfully completed by:

_____

Name of Participant

_____

Date

John R. Mergendoller, Executive Director

National Faculty

Project Based Learning for the 21st Century